ABOUT THE AUTHOR . . .

ROBERT A. WILLIAMS is presently Director of Lay Training Centers for Christian Concern Foundation, Dallas, Texas. He holds a B.A. degree from Howard Payne College, Brownwood, Texas, and B.D. and Th.M. degrees from Southwestern Baptist Theological Seminary, Fort Worth, Texas. He has pastored churches in Texas, New Mexico and Alaska.

A
PLACE
TO
BELONG

Robert A. Williams

Foreword by Cecil G. Osborne, D.D.

ZONDERVAN PUBLISHING HOUSE
A DIVISION OF THE ZONDERVAN CORPORATION
GRAND RAPIDS, MICHIGAN

A PLACE TO BELONG
© 1972 by Robert A. Williams

Library of Congress Catalog Card Number 72-183049

Scripture quotations indicated (MLB) in this book are taken from
The Modern Language Bible — The New Berkeley Version in
Modern English © 1945, 1959, 1969 by Zondervan Publishing House.
Used by permission.

Printed in the United States of America

To my wife, EVELYN,
whose calm confidence and
love
have taught me the meaning of
grace

Contents

Foreword

Acknowledgments

Preface

1. The Power of Friendship   17

2. Entering the Fellowship   29

3. The Bridge of Self-exposure   43

4. A Versatile Form   56

5. The Centered-power of Community   69

6. A Preserving Factor   80

7. The Healing Force   92

8. Feeling Private   105

9. The Indispensable Community   116

10. A Christian Availability   127

11. Dreaming Innocence   135

12. A Ministry of Listening   144

13. The Need for Creative Silence   150

14. If God Permits!   165

Foreword

This is a provocative and insightful book. The author deals with guilt, grace, forgiveness, love, and, in a most significant way, with the Church as it is and can be.

Our turbulent world, in social and moral revolution, is desperately in need of some answers. The church is searching its soul to find out where it lost the way, or at least the initiative. Why do more people look to science for answers than to Christianity? Why does the average person seek out a psychiatrist for solutions to personal problems rather than a minister?

The author of this book has, with penetrating insight, provided some answers. He is not so much a theoretician as a way-pointer.

CECIL G. OSBORNE, D.D.

Acknowledgments

So many persons have been instrumental in my writing this book that some are certain to be neglected. I can only say "thanks" to all of those who may find their influence within these pages but whose names may not appear in these acknowledgments.

My very warmest regard goes to Rev. and Mrs. Charles Logue who were instrumental in bringing me to Christ and later encouraging me in the Christian ministry. To them I owe the first chapter of this book.

A *Place to Belong* could not have been written were it not for the insights of my teacher and friend, Dr. Nat Tracy. Mutual friends who have been touched by the remarkable spiritual genius and guidance of this man will find his influence throughout the book. Both he and his "Conference on Spiritual Renewal" merit my greatest appreciation.

I am indebted, also, to all my professors at Howard Payne College, Southwestern Baptist Theological Seminary, and Baylor University for my theological education — the footing for this book. These include some twenty-five names, too numerous to practically inscribe here. A special tribute, however, goes to Dr. John P. Newport who, as my major professor, stimulated my thirst for a broadening knowledge.

I must commend the fellowships of Elm Grove Baptist Church, Placid Baptist Church, North Pole Baptist Church (Alaska), and Laos Baptist Church for offering me a place of ministry in their lives. Among these, I am extremely indebted to Charlie and Freda Carruth, Creath and Verdell Davis, Parker and Shirley George, and Nelton and Billie Merle Warren for helping me to begin my pilgrimage into the personal and for demonstrating to me the real meaning of "community."

A special note of thanks goes to Charlie and Freda Carruth for the use of their farm where this book had its beginning, and to Dr. C. O. Mitchell for the use of his farmhouse where much of the revision took place.

I am deeply grateful to the Board of Directors and Advisory Committee of Christian Concern Foundation for extending to me my present *place* of ministry as Director of the Lay Training Center. Some thirty-six couples compose this personal affirmation.

Many of the concepts in the book had their testing in Bible studies, Prayer Therapy groups (spiritual growth groups), and seminars sponsored in Arlington, Dallas, Euless, Fort Worth, McKinney, and Richardson. My appreciation goes to the participants for their humane confidence in these ideas, and for contributing many experiences that have put flesh and blood into them.

A personal word of commendation goes to Charlie and Myrna Little for serving as lay reader-consultants, to Peggy Simpkin for appraising portions of the writing, to Ray and Bettie Beltz for their encouraging friendship and help, to Rev. and Mrs. James Gibson for their contribution to my own personal well-being, and to all those of their fellowship whose struggle for reality has inspired my own.

Grateful acknowledgment also goes to the reviewers and editors of Zondervan Publishing House — especially to Bob DeVries and Al Bryant who encouraged the work all along.

A note of appreciation goes to my wife, Evelyn, and my secretary, Norma Atlason, for their concerted labor of love in preparing the final typescript.

The acknowledgments would not be complete without expressing my appreciation to Dr. Cecil Osborne for reading the manuscript and graciously consenting to write the Foreword.

Finally, I could not have endured the laborious task of writing this book without the calm confidence and love of my wife, Evelyn, to whom I dedicate these pages.

Any errors or discrepancies of thought within these pages must be attributed solely to the author and not to any of the names acknowledged above.

Preface

The decision to write this book grew out of my own struggle for a place to belong. For a long time, I have felt that of all modern entities the church should be the "living community" to offer such a place.

Whatever else may be said of the church, it must be said to be a "place" where people may feel a sense of belonging. I can remember that as children, when discussions of church attendance arose, we turned to our friends and quite unpretentiously asked the question: "Where do you belong?" We meant, of course, "Where do you 'go' to church?" or "Where are you a member?" Since we have become adults the question has not changed. Sadly enough, neither has the meaning. The meaning is still "Where do you *go?*" when it should be incisively "Where do you *belong?*"

We are not overstating the case when we observe that the emerging emphasis of the church today lies in the direction of what the New Testament calls *koinonia* (fellowship; community). The burgeoning small group movement is only one evidence. That communal groups of every imaginable nature are arising outside the church today is also obvious. The trend toward an answer to these unfulfilled longings is discernibly in motion, but it will be awhile before the church can offer the new generation an alluring, commanding fellowship.

Understandably, many of us would like to see more ideal "Christian communities" taken from the drawing board and put into motion. Invariably, as Karl Barth once put it, someone will ask us to "draw the bird flying." To do so would be to attempt the impossible. A more realistic desire would be the adventurous search, not the ordered manifestation. *Koinonia*, or the "living community of persons," is the most potent, most priceless, and most daring venture there is, and, for these reasons, also the rarest. But the principles that comprise *koinonia*, in history and on the contemporary scene, must be re-examined if "spiritual renewal" in this one area is to become a reality within Christianity. Only an honest examination can give way to the product.

This book, therefore, is not primarily a "How To" documentation on the church. Neither is it a definitive work. It is a book with struggles, invitations, and incitements. It is an attempt to convey a "spirit" of what the church ought to be.

In recent years, I have been particularly concerned with the question mark effacing the spirit of many church members. They, too, have searched for a place to belong, only to run aground on a sometimes heartless individualism. They have sought a human warmth, a fulfilling adventure, a personal affirmation, an intimate dialogue. And the church, in many cases, sponsors everything except the opening of the soul. To this question mark, this longing, the book is directed, with the hope that the readers will discover a few guidelines for making their own place and for giving the church its genuine identity.

ROBERT A. WILLIAMS

Dallas, Texas

A
PLACE
TO
BELONG

Chapter 1

The Power of Friendship

> Christianity began . . . in a vivid,
> tremendous, transforming experience
> of the friendship of Jesus. It could
> never have continued unless the
> friendship had been sustained; unless
> those who had never seen Him could
> yet enter into the fellowship and be-
> come sure of Him also.
>
> — *Leslie D. Weatherhead*

No one wanted the little half-breed boy who moved to
our community and entered the third grade with the rest
of us. Not only was he shy and reticent, but he stuttered
and had a skin color deeper than olive. Whites and Mexican
Americans predominated the little New Mexican village
where I grew up. And that is "all well and good," as they
say. But the in-between-ness of this little boy, of being both
White and Mexican, struck a jovial chord in the rest of us.
I may not have been the hero at first, but I soon ceased
my laughter — what little there was — because my heart,
by pressure not my own, went out to this young outlander.
He wanted to belong and on all sides was prevented from
belonging. Perhaps it was because I was rather frightened
of life myself that I hurt so deeply with him. I was always
reaching out for assurance, never certain I would find it.
I remember wanting to tell my dad and mother about the
personal privation of this boy, the indigence of his family.

If only I could tell them without tears. I recall mustering enough courage to persuade my mother to stop one day as we walked together past this family's home. *Maybe she would see the need*, I thought. It was all too emotional an issue for me to tell her about their circumstances. Now I wish I had told her, for we found his mother embarrassed of her furnishings and of her own appearance, looking more like a gypsy than a mother, feeling more like an alien than a neighbor.

What provoked my sensitivity was perhaps the hope I boyishly held for the underdog. Or was it? Maybe I should frankly admit that it was rather a matter of the "birds of a feather" bit. I never really understood how we got together to form such a bulwark of warmth. But then I have a hint. I have to tell you what he said to me out there beside his house one day while we played in an old abandoned, fort-like foundation. His dirty arm went around my shoulder, and he whispered something like — I forget the exact words now — "You know, you are my best friend, and I will *be* yours whether you like it or not." Beyond that, I forget all else except for a growing, encouraging companionship. He transformed me. And then he moved away.

For most of us, it is a deeply traumatic experience for individuals to "move out" of our lives. Sometimes, however, we are just as stirred by those who "move into" our lives leaving them transformed. We eventually get over the exodus of friendships that, for any number of reasons, may be snipped after they have blossomed — sometimes more temporarily as in the common move from one locality to another; sometimes more permanently as in death. But we never really get over the heritage left by the impact those friendships made as they entered our lives.

I believe that my experience with Christ and the church is based on some noble friendships I encountered as a teenager with some precisely spiritual Christians. The "church," as such, was only a place to "go" to be with my friends. They, outwardly at least, were calling themselves "Christians." But I never really "belonged" because I hardly knew what the term "Christian" meant. In fact, in my very early association with the church, I recall the minister asking the members of the congregation, from time to time, to raise their hands if they were Christians. Well, of course, I must be a "Christian," because I knew my mother had once told me that she was a member of the "Christian Church." That was enough reason to fake it with the rest. Or at least so I thought. They either had to be faking it, or there was something mighty strange about so many "Christians" (the denomination) always attending the Baptist Church.

We usually derive our impressions of others from what we see or hear. I certainly had in this case. In one of my Bible studies recently, a couple told of an enterprising dialogue taking place between two men. "Oh, you must be a Baptist," was the response of one man to something the other had said. "Close!" came the reply. "I'm an atheist!" Categorically untrue as his reply was, he had obviously determined his definition by what he had *seen* in some Baptist. What I had *heard* as a child, likewise, had been the sole determining factor for defining Christianity for me. It was a long time before I learned what it meant to be a Christian. And I had to learn it the hard way.

I was too "free-spirited" to be bound by the apron strings of the church school every Sunday. I loved the great outdoors, the adventurous Southeastern New Mexico rabbit hunts, and the Pecos River fishing holes. When my own security level was high I could let my friends ride out the Sunday drama at the church alone. But some of my friends began to have overtones of religion that seemed to be meaningful to them. I didn't know what had happened to them, and I am not sure they could fully understand it themselves. But they were persistent in trying to share it with me. They really never rubbed me the wrong way, but being individualistic, I had my pride. The minister talked a lot about being "lost" and being "saved," but that language had not even entered my vocabulary. It was all intellectually and emotionally foggy to me. And my pride, against such matters as this, outweighed my curiosity to know. In retrospect, I can see that Christ had not yet moved into my life. Then things began to change. A pastor came to our little community who took a deep interest in the youth of our junior high school — especially in the boys. Many times each week he met us on the ball field, or in the gymnasium and began relating meaningfully to us. Often, as a guest of the coach, he accompanied us on the road. Thus began the attraction of a new kind of alliance that later was to turn out particularly redemptive for many of us. This pastor and his wife began to touch our lives — from a distance at first. Then they began to meet some of our needs at a closer range, to somehow make a place for us in their home and in the church, and to give us a place in their lives. We really felt that we were important to them. And we were! More than we knew!

Not long after, the church was being filled with youth who were being drawn by the congenial qualities evident in this pastor and his wife. Many were won to the Faith and to the church. A tremendous fellowship was ballooning, but I was still faking membership in it. My heart was warming though to the sensitivity of this couple and to these friends who had made commitments to Christ. I was still unsure of what it all meant, or I might have entered sooner. Although I was beginning to be drawn more faithfully to the fellowship than many of those who were now members, months passed and I wasn't totally won. To all intents and purposes, however, no one would have suspected that I wasn't one of the bunch. All bananas look alike until you get right down to the taste. In this case, I was either a little green or a little rotten. No one really knew. But I was beginning to know — in a very disturbing way. Christ and Christianity began to bug me. I wanted to know what it was all about. I wanted to understand, because I was beginning to be understood.

My teenage friends were all seeking a place. Many had

found one by surrender. But my shell of rugged individualism — or was it sophisticated pride? — was a hard one to
crack. Christianity was a paradox to me — I wanted it and
I didn't. I have since learned that it was the sin-spirit of
rebellion in me that created this paradox and prevented my
coming to Christ at the outset. Not knowing this then,
however, I had to be *won* to the Faith like all the rest. And
it was the winning spirit of my friends that finally got me.

Once during a revival meeting in our little community
church, I had to face the reality of the demands being placed
upon me by these persistent peers. My pretense was being
seriously threatened about this time. During Sunday school
one morning, our teacher, who happened to be the pastor's
wife, requested that we close our class session with prayer
for a certain list of individuals she held in her hand. "Pray
for them," she suggested, "that they might come to a face-
to-face encounter with Christ during this revival." With
those words she began to read the list. When she came
to *my name* I was stunned. What could I do now, I thought.
They have discovered me. All I could do was what I had
been doing all along — so I faked it as always! But how
do you fake your own *presence* among friends who are praying for you specifically by name? You know how! Act as
if you didn't hear. Walk out laughing and talking with
them unassumingly. Cover up in the crowd to distract attention. So I did — and I escaped momentarily.

You never really escape that easily, though, so I cowered
further by concealing myself among the choir members. That
was an uncalculated mistake! Christ encountered me there,
too, in the person of another friend. Following the service
and my attempt to screen myself from the sermon and all
else that might unmask me, I proceeded from the choir loft.
But a soft hand clasped my shoulder and I surrendered long
enough to hear the whisper: "I am praying for you." Never
had I looked at a girl so helplessly, so washed out.

A few weeks later, in the privacy of my own room about
midnight, I cut the Gordian knot that had constricted me,

and Christ entered my life. Lying on my bunk, I prayed (in retrospect) something like: "Lord, I hardly understand You. My friends are assured that You are there, but I don't understand all they say. I am mixed up and lonely. I don't even know what it is they want me to do. But whatever it means to be 'saved,' whatever it means to be a 'Christian,' if You are there, meet me tonight and enter my life." With that prayer the stronghold of pretense collapsed and a whole cargo of relief rushed in. I fell asleep — once an insurgent, now restored. All seemed quiet now.

I learned from this experience that God will *begin* with a person in his most elemental and illiterate stages; but I learned, too, that no man really enters the kingdom of God alone. I thought I had, in that I was now "in the kingdom" but was taking my time in committing myself to church membership as a new convert. I was not even declaring my profession. Had I not struggled through my own predicament, answered my own inner quest, changed my own existential setting? I might have liked having it that way. But there is no feigning the tremendous impact of friendship that, in the very beginning, intrigued me and finally won me.

This personal heritage teaches me a very enterprising lesson, never to be forgotten: *that there is a certain charisma about friendship, a certain transforming charm.* Probably the best example of this, contemporaneous with our age, came out of the Billy Graham Greater London Crusade in 1954. Graham's critics at the outset were certainly not few in number. One of his more caustic detractors was "Cassandra" (William Connor), columnist of the London *Daily Mirror*. Following a face-to-face meeting with Graham in a London pub, and finding him as genuine as thousands hold him to be, Cassandra wrote in his column the next day: "I never thought that friendliness had such a sharp cutting edge. I never thought that simplicity could cudgel us sinners so damned hard." [1]

---

[1] Clarence W. Hall, "The Charisma of Billy Graham," *Reader's Digest* (July, 1970), p. 92.

I have had a feeling since those early years when I began to know the meaning of Christianity, that the rise of the early church must have had its staging in the charisma of Christ. Anyone who reads the gospels seriously has to be struck by His winsomeness. He moved men profoundly by His extraordinary power of friendship. I recall the first time I viewed the movie "Ben Hur," and saw the personal magnetism of Christ portrayed on the screen. I was moved to tears and driven to see it again the following week. I have seen it twice since and never cease to marvel at the tremendous impact it makes on the sensitive heart. Because the movie is so penetratingly real to the character of Christ, I have been on a spiritual marathon with Him ever since. My chief love of the New Testament, in fact, is in thinking in terms of His character. When I read His personal dialogues with the common man, or with the magistrates, or with His more religious contemporaries, and then read the long history of the church, I am drawn to one conclusion: *to attribute the rise of the church to any other motive power quite as awesome as the remarkable, transforming friendship of Christ is unthinkable.*

There was something extremely attractive about Christ; about the manner in which He affected life. At first sight, He appeared to men as strangely human and only divine as they began to perceive an unchampioned quality of character rising to the surface. Men sought the choicest human categories into which to place Him and none were suitable. They looked to history's heroes and none were resplendent enough to answer His question — "Who do men say that I am?" Some said He was Elijah, a strong prophet of the past, returned from the grave. Maybe they had seen His indignant flares of anger in such instances as when He cleansed the Temple of money changers, or when He prescribed a millstone for the cure of child-offenders.

And yet, this wasn't the full story of His character. On another occasion His disciples were eager for Him to call down fire from heaven and consume His hecklers, but His spirit was more engaging and sympathetic. Others said He might be the virile Essene, John the Baptist — perhaps because John was the first prophet of true greatness for four hundred years, and Christ appeared to have the same message: "The kingdom of God is at hand!"

Still others said He was more like Jeremiah, the "weeping prophet" — perhaps because of the great tenderness that dominated His life. The word surely had gotten around that "Jesus wept." Someone had overheard Him weeping over Jerusalem because He had succored Israel like a hen her brood, and they were not moved.

Yet again, others, perhaps by blind guess alone, generalized and said He was one of the other prophets. Men just did not grasp easily His true greatness. Outrightly He had to tell that segment of His own generation who rejected Him: "The men of Nineveh shall arise against this nation at the judgment and condemn you. For when Jonah preached to them, they repented and turned to God from all their evil ways. And now *a greater than Jonah is here* — and you refuse to believe Him. The Queen of Sheba shall rise against this nation in the judgment, and condemn it; for she came from a distant land to hear the wisdom of Solomon; and now *a greater than Solomon is here* — and you refuse to believe Him."[2]

It was only after most of His ministry had transpired, that, finally at Caesarea Philippi, one man, Simon Peter, caught the true picture of His character. Against that silhouette, that design, almost in soliloquy now and under his breath, Simon blurted from within: "Thou art the Christ, the Son of the living God." At last one man and God were in harmony over the personality of Christ, for flesh and blood had not revealed this truth to Simon.

I marvel at the contagion of Christ's out-going manner. Men were so enamored by His character that some of them went too far in their attempt to be like Him and soon were

[2] Matthew 12:41, 42 *(The Living Bible)*, Tyndale House, Wheaton, Ill. Italics are mine.

saying dangerously, "I am the Christ."[3] Many false messiahs thus arose to vindicate their aspirations and their pride. But more challenging than all were those who were drawn to Him for right reasons, like slivers of steel to some magnetic pole.

His spirit of optimism was like a disease. And that may be as humorous as it is piercing; for men contracted His positive disposition much as they would smallpox or fever — it fairly rubbed off on them.

Nowhere else in history, ancient or contemporary, do we see life so extremely commanding as in His enjoyment of its common ventures. He still holds, unchallenged, the master key to the art of living. I am deeply moved at His sanctioning of marriage and social gatherings by attending the wedding in Cana of Galilee. He put the deep, red burgundy of joy back into life and symbolized that aspect in the character of God by changing the water into wine. He so oriented Himself with winebibbers, who wanted to go straight, that men called Him one. He joked with the woman of Canaan about feeding the children's bread to the dogs, and she felt free to join in the irony. Strange thing, isn't it — His favorite method of teaching was by the simple use of the parable. Nothing better describes just how close to life He was, enjoying all the common events, and drawing from them lessons that bore the marks of eternity.

A whole spate of general qualities hover in His life that draw me into alliance with Him. *He met with weak and unimportant people and gave them strength and determination* — and I desperately need that kind of strength. *He met with the perverse and hostile and revealed a poise that made Him approachable* — and my security level is such that I must never be repelled by Him. He cannot be pious or remote and have my heart. *He sat down with the unlovely and the unloved and made them lovers like Himself* — and I yearn to blossom into His kind of caring. I refuse to be a forgotten man, and hope none will be forgotten because of

[3] See Matthew 24:5, 24 and 1 John 4:1-3.

me. *The quality and depth of His life made Him tolerant and understanding* — and more than all else I need to be understood and forgiven. *He was desperately sensitive and open to the hurt of men.* Whenever they were beaten, cheated, or oppressed, it wounded His heart and raised His indignation.

Men called for help and received it; others received it without a summons — and I am drawn to that kind of chivalry. Most perceptible of all was the dominant quality of His life: *He was vividly more interested in others than He was in Himself.* He considered their welfare the destiny of His life, and it was the assumption of this destiny in an unselfish extension of Himself to men that *transformed* their lives. No one could deny the affirming quality of His recruiting friendship — and I feel even now that I am standing in the shadows of a new kind of *koinonia.*

If you ask me to diagnose scientifically how the *koinonia* of Christ changed men, I cannot tell you. I see no pattern of curricula to follow, no simple rules to trust. But I am determined that if we could walk with Jesus Christ for one day, we would sense a measurable transformation. Albert Einstein, scientific genius though he was, could only respond by declaring: "I am enthralled by the luminous figure of the Nazarene!" And that is all we can say, too. Men were simply drawn to Him because He opened His life to them as a gift, befriended them, forgave them. Out of this spirit came transformation and the rise of the Christian community. Weatherhead was therefore strikingly apt when he wrote: "Christianity began then in a vivid, tremendous, transforming experience of the friendship of Jesus. It could never have continued unless the friendship had been sustained; unless those who had never seen Him could yet enter into the fellowship and become sure of Him also." [4]

The transforming experience of the friendship of Christ is both sustaining and assuring, because it is strangely con-

[4] Leslie D. Weatherhead, *The Transforming Friendship* (London: The Epworth Press, 1928), p. 51.

temporary. Let me explain. Some months ago I had lunch with a charming friend, who was brim-full of some new movings-of-God in her life. "It all started one day," she said, "when I asked myself, 'Why am I on dead-center? God is really doing nothing important in my life. Why?' And then I saw that I was on dead-center because *I was not moving.*" She went on to share how God was beginning to open up a new sense of her usefulness to her family and to other people. She was beginning to affect deeply some of the relationships she was encountering. More than ever she was beginning to get outside herself. As she bubbled over with this new enthusiasm, she began to weep. There in the restaurant, tears of joy streamed down her face.

And I thought within — *There is no greater beauty in the world than the weakness of a woman desiring to be heard for all the meaning in her life.* I interjected: "You really must be full!"

She wiped her tears in affirmation and continued, "You know, I am beginning to see the meaning of real servant-hood. God is beginning to be so real." She then recalled some wisdom from a mutual friend, my own teacher for a number of years. "He often told us," she remembered, "that *reality always answers back.*" Trying to express the reverberation of a real God to the question of life, she went on to recall a recent struggle over the near-death of her father-in-law. "There I stood helplessly before his bed," she remarked, "not knowing if . . . " [and silence momentarily settled over her as if to conclude] ". . . if he would make it or not." Then with the tears brushed away once more she added: "But something strange came over me and I felt a Presence. *I knew I was not alone, and I knew He was my Friend!*"

I was impelled to share with her a similar experience of my own just a week before. I had begun the first night of a home Bible study on the "Life and Character of Christ." For some reason, I felt the need for some affirmation that God was really with the group that evening. In the opening prayer I asked the Christ of our study to walk in among us and be our spiritual guest. I do not know what the others felt, but fifteen minutes into the session I felt strangely warmed by the truth that was being shared. Overcome momentarily, with a lump in my throat, tears in my eyes, I had to stop. I could not go on until I had asked for a glass of water from the host and had sat a moment, as if I were waiting for this Friend to be seated. In a moment I continued — with the living Christ among us. The power of His transforming presence was, as my friend had said, "reality answering back." And as I have thought about it again and again, I have not changed my mind. It *was!* And it *is!*

Chapter 2

Entering the Fellowship

> If one seeks fellowship, he
> must extend fellowship.
> — *Edward J. Carnell*

A few years ago, I sat in a classroom listening to my teacher centering in on the Cross and Resurrection experiences of Christ. Following class I found a quiet place in the library where I could think through his imposing propositions. Still under the spell of his words, I listened again as my mind wandered back into history. In a moment I was asking myself pointedly: "Suppose you had stood at the foot of the cross and watched Jesus die. With Him apparently defeated, would you have been able to convince yourself, now that it was all over, that you could furnish His kind of alliance to the world?" The more I mused, the more I became sure of the answer — "No, it is very doubtful." I could see myself standing there no different from those who stood beside me. I was first fearful, then dejected, now even skeptical. Yet, with them, I was under promise and commission to carry the gospel to the ends of the earth.

Then in my imagination I came to that splendid moment of the Resurrection, and the whole picture began to change. I was the onlooker this time rather than the participant, and I saw how those people could be sure of Christ.

The drama was very convincing. Without the fact of the

Resurrection, the Christian community would have fallen stillborn from its gestation in the dreams of Christ, for Christ seemed to have surrendered the whole mosaic, dreams and all, when He submitted to His death. Except for the added "appearances" of the risen Christ to reassure the despairing followers that He was both alive and the "same Jesus," the Christian community might never have been born and certainly not sustained. Here were some lonely people who, upon the death of their Leader, did not know where to turn. Some of them, His disciples, out of both fear and disappointment, had fled Him when the pressure was on, and many of the rest were too melancholic for any life-asserting movement to begin in them. But three days later, something tremendously explosive happened. The Man who had perfectly embodied *koinonia* came back from the dead.

Ordinary men would not have returned to such a whipping boy spirit; a spirit which, in this case, was saying, "We are the fellowship of the forsaken." Nor would they have returned to a fellowship in which weakness had led to desertion. But life began to revive when the *living* Christ stepped from the shadows into the sunlight, for He went looking for those who had forsaken Him. When He found them, He extended to them, again, the fellowship they had known before, but with the added assurance that it was *permanent.* Those who entered the fellowship a second time found themselves entering a relationship that carried eternal weight, both for themselves and for the world. Now came the confidence that in fellowship with Christ they could make it, because He had — and not only could make it, but could also help furnish that kind of relationship to the world.

The church, therefore, was to have been, in essence, *the sustaining friendship of Christ embodied in a people.* As a *koinonia,* it was to have been such a magnificent relationship of belonging that others entering it could be sure of Christ too.

The need for this kind of assurance is the reason why the early community placed so much stress on eyewitness accounts. The four gospels, Matthew, Mark, Luke and John, were, in fact, the first "Christian apologetics" to guarantee the veracity of the Christian world view. Christianity was not a closed issue by any means. Many philosophies were rampant that would have undercut the central truth that Jesus of Nazareth was the incarnate Son of God. Consequently, the two daring ideas that John wanted to defend, when he wrote his first epistle, was that Jesus Christ was a *real* man, not a *phantom*, so described by the Gnostic cult, and that men could enter into fellowship with Him. John selected a whole raft of sensory words to defend the humanity of Christ, and then wisely used the first person plural ("we" and "us") to give the whole argument the support of a *community witness*. Into that kind of veracity he could now invite others. There is something settling about his appeal:

> It is what existed from the beginning, what we have seen with our own eyes, what we have beheld, what our hands have touched, about the very message of life — and that life has been unveiled to us, and we have seen it and now testify to it and we now announce it to you, yea, the eternal life that was with the Father and has been unveiled to us. I repeat, it is what we have seen and heard that we now announce to you, so that you *too may share this fellowship with us,* for this fellowship that we have is with the Father and with His Son Jesus Christ. [1]

The real hope for the church today will lie in its ability to offer a new quality of relationship to this generation. Whatever else the relationship will be it will have to be as explosive as the one Christ offered His generation. Paul, writing to the Christians at Rome, admonished: "Therefore, practice receiving one another into full Christian fellowship, just as Christ has so received you to Himself." [2] The admoni-

---

[1] 1 John 1:1-3 (C. B. Wms.). Italics are mine.
[2] Romans 15:7 (C. B. Wms.).

tion by the late Edward J. Carnell is as prominently germane: "If one seeks fellowship, he must extend fellowship." [3]

What kind of relationship must the fellowship of Christ present to the world if it expects the world to enter into its alliance? A number of attitudes seem apparent, which will make the relationship one of unity and belonging for all who enter it.

First, the church must be a *fellowship of affirmation*. In his book, *The Healing Partnership*, Bernard Steinzor writes: "The person with a strong ego who actualizes his potential cannot become so without the affirmation of 'significant others.' And, furthermore, he cannot continue to affirm his creative possibilities unless he finds at least one other person who continues to affirm his being." [4] The community of Christ of all people should be the most supportive group in the world. In many cases it is not.

In a recent *koinonia* group composed of interested seminary students, an entire year was given to the sharing of lives and to understanding the reality of Jesus Christ and the Christian calling. More than once the question of the contemporary church arose, and invariably the students became disgruntled, if not irate, with their own churches for not pursuing the more personal value of a supportive fellowship. In almost every case the contention was against the churches biding their time on the more functional and mundane elements of organizational pursuits. These students were not looking for a dainty, well-organized place to which they could come for pulling the church wagon, or keeping its program on the road, however well-meaning. More than all else they were intensely in need of coming to grips with their own inner life. They were looking for a body of people who would serve them at the point of their deepest need — the need to be affirmed, to find some kind of support for their

[3] Edward J. Carnell, *Christian Commitment* (New York: The Macmillan Company, 1957), p. 55.

[4] Bernard Steinzor, *The Healing Partnership* (New York: Harper & Row, Publishers, 1967), p. 245.

struggles, to have their motivation in life restored by knowing that they really were significant after all.

By affirmation is not meant the mere pat-on-the-back syndrome. Rather, it is chiefly a supportive attitude that, at its core, is positive instead of negative. All of us know the feeling that comes when someone, rather than merely flattering us, affirms us by mentioning some positive quality in us. We all need to receive affirmation and we all need to give it — mainly because all of us have an insatiable drive to belong. Two personal experiences may help to describe this basic need for mutual optimism.

One is the time I went home with a college girl friend, and for the first time, was privileged to meet her sister just younger than she. I had been forewarned that she was a beautiful girl and that I should brace myself for the eventful shock to come. When I saw her, she was everything I had heard and more. Really so overwhelmed by it all, I had an impulse to tell her that I thought she was very beautiful and quite everything her sister had described. I was *giving* affirmation, which seemed at the time very appropriate. But just as impulsively she countered from behind a twelve-pound look: "Don't flatter yourself!" I was sincere in my compliment, but she was unable to *receive* it.

The other incident happened only recently in one of my Bible studies. A charming lady in the group was sharing openly some of her recent struggles and joys in her Christian pilgrimage. She momentarily turned to me and offered a compliment that affirmed my ministry in the group as much as anything could have. Calling me by name she remarked: "You are one minister with whom I do not feel inferior." I acknowledged her compliment with a passing "Thank you." But the affirmation was not passing. She was *giving* affirmation, which a few years ago I would have taken rather grimly, for I wanted to feel "superior" in every instance. But now it was the finest compliment she could have paid me. Those who are not ministers may not know how lonely one may become by such unintentional remarks as: "Oh, he's a preacher," or "So you are the 'good' pastor from so and so."

Members of the Christian community have to learn sensitivity in this area of affirmation. Do outsiders know by our attitude that we are *for* them? Do they know that they will be sincerely welcomed and not indubitably offended — even if they are prostitutes or have prison records?

Nothing speaks to the disconsolate, the weak, the lonely, or even the wretched quite as powerfully as the reality of one who is wilfully reaching out to others. No cutting edge is sharper than "acceptance" to those who normally fear rejection. Even the most casual experiences of acceptance and optimism in our relationships give us the consolation that someone is *with us*.

I received a letter from a dear friend after being on a retreat with her at Kaleo Lodge in East Central Texas. She had been struggling with some minor issues in her life — if indeed any struggle is ever minor — and had become more decisive in her feelings toward them. In the letter she said: "Thanks for putting me at ease. I feel I'm me with you — just mean old me — and it's okay with you."

A couple in another state who had gone through one of the spiritual growth groups wrote my wife and me. I did not know how powerful "affirmation" could really be until I read their heartening words. Their concluding remark in the letter was: "We want to express our appreciation for the interest you both have taken in us. Your friendship means much to us. We know that there are at least two people in the world who accept us unconditionally." Their friendship and affirmation had been a boon to our lives as well. We had been changed by their kindness.

Before this couple moved from our city, the husband had drawn me aside one day to express his confidence. He had received fifty dollars from a lady in his home town who requested that he give it to someone in the seminary who could really use it. I am not being facetious when I say that he could have walked into the hall and slipped the money into the hands of the first passer-by and have instantly fulfilled her request. Every seminary student I have ever known could have used that fifty dollars.

But my friend chose me. He took me out on the front steps, invited me to sit down, and then the story began. When the mission was accomplished, I felt that I was the richest person on the campus — not because I had fifty dollars, but because I had someone sitting next to me who could have used the money himself but who was more interested in *my* welfare than his own. Here was observable evidence, embodied in a person, that the friendship of Christ had been sustained.

As I have studied the life of Christ, I have asked myself, "What is the one characteristic that stands out above all others in His life?" Is it not that He gave everyone He met a sense of their significance by offering them a place in His life? It may be true, in varying degrees, that to the hungry He was bread, to the sick He was health, to the dead, in some instances, He was resuscitation. But to everyone, fevered or whole, responsive or callowed, He was *affirmation.* He never met a man for whom there was not a place in His heart. And it showed! Men knew it! They felt wanted, needed, valued. Although He responded to their need, He never calculated nor demanded their response — but He usually got it, for no one else reacted so sensitively to their feelings of alienation and loneliness, their desperate thirst for belonging.

You learn many things from those who have become patients in the back wards of mental hospitals and from those who work with them. In one instance, as our study group toured the hospital the supervisors told us about their "Intensive Push Program." The therapeutic attitude most beneficial to these patients was what is known among psychiatrists as "reinforcement." It is much akin to the word "affirmation" in the way in which I have been using it. "Reinforcement" is a "non-verbal reward gesture" toward the patients. In two instances it opened up an atmosphere of "trust."

One patient, a chronic alcoholic, was given a job in a local saloon. We were told that at break time the patient would go to the bar and have his usual Coca Cola. He was rewarded, or "reinforced" by being trusted with his job and given daily freedom from the hospital.

In the other instance, we were told that a patient had been a frequent runaway and could be dangerous to himself and others. Yet under the new system he was given the key to his ward and was responsible for admitting and excusing patients who went to their daily chores on the hospital grounds. We were then informed that this patient, since that time, amazingly had never run away. "Reinforcement" had given him a significant place as the doorman.

Second, the church must be a *fellowship of the forgiven.* Although I want to deal with this aspect more in detail in a later chapter, a brief mention of it here is essential. Those in the fellowship who know they have been forgiven and actually have accepted that forgiveness from God by forgiving themselves, ought then to offer the same generosity to others who need it. If they do not feel forgiven themselves, chances are they will not know how to forgive. Christ said, "To whom little is forgiven, the same loveth little." [5] Again He said, "Unto whomsoever much is given, of him shall be much required." [6] When forgiveness can be offered generously, as Christ set forth in these principles, a remarkable sense of relief comes over the one forgiven.

I remember a classmate of mine (whom I shall call Jay for the sake of anonymity) who shared a painful experience with me. He and his wife had been visited by a distant relative their own age. The relative was a beautiful girl, and in little ways during the stay she made it apparent that she was attracted to Jay. It was left to him on the final night of the visit to take her to the bus depot. Waiting for con-

[5] Luke 7:47 (k.j.v.).
[6] Luke 12:48 (k.j.v.).

nections, with time on their hands, they decided to take a drive around town. One thing led to another and finally they were on a country road with intentions. Something awakened in him, however, and the final act was not committed, but a swath of guilt flooded his life and he later had to confide in someone — someone who might understand. He felt that I might, for which I am grateful. We talked a long time that evening, and then we joined in contrition under the light of God's forgiveness. As best I knew how to forgive, I reached out unconditionally and offered him my heart and my hand — and he received them with joy. Although he has since moved away, I shall never forget the benefit one receives in forgiving and being forgiven.

Neither shall I forget the sheer beauty of tears, sparkling with the joy of forgiveness, that flowed freely in one of our spiritual growth groups. One of the ladies told her story of how as a child she had been deprived of love and acceptance. During these early years a relative, somewhat older than she, took advantage of her sexually and in her innocence she had mistaken this as an expression of endearment. "I actually loved it," she said amidst sobs, "because I felt wanted." But later as she matured, she began to develop a sense of guilt over this early involvement. All these years until this particular night she had carried that burden, afraid to tell anyone. But now, among friends who deeply cared for her, she revealed her feelings and told her story. We sat in silence and sobbed with her as the relief of forgiveness swept in upon us.

Surely you will agree that we could use a great many "fellowships" that can *hurt* when another hurts, and *sob* when another sobs, and *forgive* because they know what it means to be forgiven.

Third, the church must be a *fellowship of suffering*. By this expression I do not mean that the church will be a hospital for the physically infirm. The church was never meant to be an infirmary; not even a place for shot-in-the-arm religion or pep-pill dramas to tide men over a week.

And although the church *must be concerned deeply* about the cancer victim, the coronary patient, the aged and the dying, it must recognize also, that men ail on a deeper level than the physical. Certainly these are in pain, but their spirits are in trouble, too. Emotionally, spiritually, they grasp for support. Their cry is: "Does anyone *care* that I suffer? Does anyone *know* the desperation of my soul?" The church ought to know! And the church ought to care!

A portion of Paul's great prayer to Christ for himself reads: "That I may know him, and the power of his resurrection, and the *fellowship of his sufferings*, being made conformable unto his death." [7] By this Paul meant that he wanted to share in the vicarious nature of Christ. If only he could in some way help to alleviate pain, struggle with men through their sufferings, take part of their load and shoulder it himself — that is his appeal. To the Colossians he wrote: "I am now glad to be suffering for you, and in my own person I am filling in what is lacking in Christ's suffering for His body, that is, the church." [8] "Filling in what is lacking" does not mean that Christ's death lacked something, and that Paul, in his own body, would now complete that suffering. But it does mean that he wanted to participate in Christ's burden for the world.

One of the objectives of Christ, in fact, is to produce a "body" of people, the church, who will help carry out His tremendous plan for the world by sharing in His burden for it. Christ means to make us moral saviors in the sense that something of His own healing spirit will enter our lives so others may find support in their afflictions. As the church, we are to be His saving people who will elevate that part of the world which we touch.

Paul's prayer then, and its practical fulfillment in the church, is the secret of the great life. Those who abandon themselves to the hurt of other men have to be the nobility among us. Christ said: "Whosoever will be *chief* among you,

[7] Philippians 3:10 (K.J.V.). Italics are mine.
[8] Colossians 1:24 (C. B. Wms.).

let him be your servant: even as the Son of man came not to be ministered unto, but to minister, and to give his life *a ransom for many.*" [9] To have our lives polarized in Jesus Christ means to engage in vicarious suffering on behalf of others. Hopefully, the impact of Christ upon our lives will bring us to the place where we will even pray as Paul prayed, knowing as he knew that it is "Christ in you the hope of your glorification." [10]

In my imagination I nurse a fond hope that one day Christ will bring me to the place where I can respond to the Father in this way: "Oh, God, I see your burden, your endless concern and suffering for the whole world. May I, in a measure, participate in that burden? Give me this man who stands nearby, who strives despairingly. Let me minister to him, serve him, and lighten his load — and that will be enough."

I keep coming back to the Pole-star of the universe, Jesus Christ, to capture the guiding light of His passion for men. His great soliloquy in the eleventh chapter of Matthew is among His warmest words and reveals His remarkable vicarious nature. He has just upbraided some of the chief centers of religion (Chorazin, Bethsaida, Capernaum) because they had seen His mighty works and were not moved. He had not been long in His first great ministry and already it appeared that He was losing ground. But at this point He recognizes that the strategy of the Father has been correct — the things of God have been hidden to those who are wise and prudent in their own eyes, but open to babes, who by nature have remained teachable. He realizes, too, that the burden of the world has been delivered to Him by the Father, and that is more striking still. In one somber moment He looks across the desperate human race and knows that He must assume its moral burden. Looking into the distance His heart breaks, and in soliloquy He whispers

---

[9] Matthew 20:27, 28 (k.j.v.). Italics are mine.
[10] Colossians 1:27 (C. B. Wms.).

within: "Come unto me, all *ye* that labour and are heavy
laden, and I will give you rest. Take my yoke upon you,
and learn of me; for I am meek and lowly in heart: and ye
shall find rest unto your souls. For my yoke *is* easy, and my
burden is light." [11]

Assuming that kind of burden, or at least part of it, is
precisely Paul's plea later and should be the aspiration of
God's people today. But such intensity of life immediately
causes us to balk. "How will the burden of the world,"
we ask, "keep from being overbearing? Will it not burden
us down and sap our energy?" And the answer is "yes,"
until we realize that we are not alone in it. We are invited
into Christ's yoke *with Him,* to learn from Him. He had the
support of the Father all along. His yoke was easy and His
burden light because God was in it with Him. And He is
with us no less.

I grasp the symbolism more accurately when I recall my
grandfather's farming days. Until retirement, he farmed
all his land with mules. When he broke in a new mule he
sometimes had difficulty training it for the traces. A mule
fresh out of the mountains did not respond well to the pull
of the reins, much less understand the "Gee" and "Haw"
of a man's voice. But my grandfather knew how to solve
the problem. He placed the new mule in the traces alongside one fully trained and tempered. The new mule could
now *learn* from the one seasoned in the art.

For us to place ourselves in the yoke alongside Christ will
allow us to *learn* from the One who knew how to bear the
burden of the world. Christ once symbolized His servanthood by washing His disciples' feet. He then turned to
them and said: "I have given you an *example*, that you
should do as I have done to you." [12]

To be a *fellowship* of suffering lends much support in
burden bearing. The value of *koinonia* is that we can bear

[11] Matthew 11:28-30 (K.J.V.).
[12] John 13:15 (K.J.V.).

one anothers' burdens, and thus fulfill the law of Christ — the law of love and servanthood. [13] This quality of vicariously opening oneself to the struggles of another has happened in many of our spiritual growth groups. But one that stands out foremost in my mind brings the matter home most convincingly. Here is the witness, in detail, of a lovely lady who entered one of our groups. Entering it she entered a new kind of fellowship, one that met her at the point of her deepest struggles. She writes:

When I entered the group, I had been living in a state of almost continual depression, feeling little desire to work at letting the Holy Spirit control my life. I did not realize it fully, but I was full of hostility, feelings of insecurity, despair, and hopelessness in many ways. I had in some ways "given up." My only hope was in the thought of one day being in heaven, away from my complicated circumstances. I needed to share my feelings with someone, but I did not know how to do this.

The first time I attended the group and listened to what we would be doing, something leaped to life in my heart, and I knew that here God could show me what I needed to do to allow Him to heal my life. Later, as I began getting my slips (analysis of the tests) and praying about them, knots or chains began to be loosed inside. Of course some of the searching was very painful and depressing temporarily, but guidance from *Prayer Can Change Your Life, The Art of Understanding Yourself*, and comments in the group helped me see that I could put the past straight and yield the present to God.

After four months of work in the group I know that I am not a completely healthy personality, but I'm much better. And the best thing is that I have hope for improving in the months ahead. My family sees a difference and I feel a difference. I'm not afraid to look at myself anymore. Life has more challenge in it, and I love my family and friends in a deeper way. Relationships seem more important now, and I do not fear them.

[13] Galatians 6:2.

Into the hothouse climate of true community, persons can enter and *find rootage.* They can easily commit their lives to a fellowship of affirmation because it meets their insatiable drive to belong. They can honorably give themselves to a fellowship of the forgiven because it dissolves their guilt feelings without making them feel inferior. And they can enter heartily into a fellowship of suffering because they know, awaiting them, there is support for their most crucial crises. In this kind of explosive relationship they can discover their growing-edge to wholeness and be impelled in the expanding adventure of life with Jesus Christ. Now, because they know the preciousness of being cherished as worthy participants in the human race, they can, in turn, bring healing to the shambles of life around them.

Chapter 3

The Bridge of Self-exposure

> It is apparent that honesty
> and integrity are the universal
> starting place for spiritual life
> and renewal.
>
> — *Nat Tracy*

Everyone has the right to reveal or conceal himself. He has the right to secrets which in all probability should never go on parade. Therefore, asking someone to expose himself is like verbally confronting him. You are inviting a battle in either case. *He* may pull off the mask but *you* had better not. For you to expose him becomes a most serious form of exploitation.

But there is a healthy kind of self-exposure which does not end in "exhibitionism." It is a life of openness and integrity, a life of candid, transparent character — an exposure of the innermost self to the world.

At heart, each of us responds to the kind of plea that Katherine Mansfield left us in her *Letters to John Middleton Murray* — "If I were allowed one single cry to God, that cry would be: 'I want to be real'." [1] Such a plea is a big order, not easily filled, but somewhere there is a start in that direction.

A simple test will show us how difficult the task really

[1] Katherine Mansfield, *Letters to John Middleton Murray* (New York: Alfred A. Knopf, 1951), p. 697.

may be. At least it will be a beginning. For a single day write down all the phony idiosyncrasies that occur in your relationships. List the times you tell someone a half-truth because you feel he will be none the wiser or simply in order to save face. Note the times you deliberately or perhaps even unconsciously, attempt to impress someone. Add to this your overly affected conversations in which you either exaggerate your circumstances or stress your own "perfections." It is evident that to go on listing all our personal, social quirks and profane ways of living would only be time consuming.

When we tally the list at the end of the day, one fact is instantly observable — we cannot live even for one day without lying to ourselves and others. And although we do not live above deception, we act as if we can and do. We look within and around us and admit that this really is a dollhouse world, just as play-like as it can be, but we have the suspicious feeling all along that it wouldn't be nearly as difficult if "you" believed in "me."

If we were more honest, we might be more believable. That is what I hear among people exchanging personal views. More especially, that is what I hear the world saying to the church — "If you lived up to your profession, we might believe in you."

As a pastor the most frequent excuse for not attending the church services that I heard was: "Oh, I would come to church if it were not so full of hypocrites!" To answer that excuse demanded very little mental energy. Those who offered it did not know that this was precisely why we were going to church. We knew we were hypocrites — inwardly divided, self-deceptive beings. We knew that our lives were not always on the up-and-up, much less on the level. We needed a fellowship to handle the discrepancies in our lives. We believed that the church was the training ground for producing open people. Moreover, we hoped that once we learned openness together, we could better extend it to others as a *bridge* over which they could cross into our lives.

Maybe we didn't learn very well (reason enough for the excuse), but there is not much difference between an out-and-out "hypocrite" and a person who makes the pathetic claim that he is not theatrical like the rest of us. "If we say that we have no sin, we deceive ourselves, and the truth is not in us."[2]

Admittedly, one of the major trouble spots of Christianity in our day is the inability of the church to affect society deeply. A few years ago in the county in which I then lived, there were approximately 800 churches. Of that number 170 were of my own denomination. For all our numerical efficiency, we were not making a dent in the character of society at large.

I began to question. Why is the church not more impelling? Why does it languish? Why is life within not more nobly impressive to men on the outside? I felt there had to be an answer if Jesus Christ were Head of the church.

Part of the answer came as I looked back to the early Christian community and sought the "norm" of its life. I wanted to know the common denominator that seemed to characterize its witness. I listed a conglomerate of vital characteristics that might win any heart; but a closer look turned up a point common to each. For instance, I saw men who had self-centeredness broken in them — but not totally; men who were living a radiant life of joy — but not always; men who demonstrated Christ-centered qualities — but not entirely; men who kept the Law more as internalized principles than as external rules — but not perfectly; men who bore love, acceptance, and forgiveness — but not unalloyed; men who were involved in what they professed — but not in every instance; and men who appeared to be free — but not fully. Here was my answer! None were ivory saints. None gave the sacerdotal impression. *These men were capable of genuine openness.* If they were in the least wayward, they could admit to it. The *ideal* always gave way

[2] 1 John 1:8 (K.J.V.).

to the *human* in them, but the dichotomy was never covered over as though it did not exist. Hence, because they did not think themselves so superb, outsiders were not repelled by them. I concluded that men could cross over a bridge of integrity.

Did this mean that I could be honest? That I could be consistent? I certainly was hopeful. If the writers of the New Testament recorded the embarrassing about themselves and the Christian community, why must I cover up? Quickly the answer came. Because I am insecure! I must be accepted. I have to belong.

As a Christian teenager I remember one foolish event in my life that shattered my hope for being morally consistent. Riding home on the school bus one evening, I sat next to a girl I wanted to date. I thought she wanted to date me, too, until I asked. She was already dating a boy in our village — and quite seriously, I gathered. Feeling my oats, I decided to challenge her answer. But the issue was settled.

Peeved by her determination and the threat to my masculinity, I countered with a belittling remark about the boy's family. With that it was losers weepers all the way — especially the following day. The family had been told; my pastor had heard; and someone had mentioned that the boyfriend was looking for me.

At first I denied my guilt. It was too painful for me to admit that I had been so impulsive toward a family I deeply loved. It was that old slip of the tongue bit, and I was in too deeply to back out casually. After my pastor spoke to me about it, I knew what had to be done. I had to make amends, but I was trembling with fright at the thought.

When a group of my friends understood the motive involved, they sympathized by escorting me to the family's home. With their support, amidst a roomful of tears, I was able to concede my blunder and to ask forgiveness. The breach was healed. Delightfully, I learned that they liked me better as an "open" sinner than as a "lying" saint. (Incidentally, the boy and girl went on to fall in love and marry. I wish them God's richest blessing.)

I am relieved later in life to find that even the Apostle Paul struggled with the problem of moral inconsistency. He said: "I keep under my body, and bring *it* into subjection: lest that by any means, when I have preached to others, I myself should be a castaway." [3] His chief fear was that he might become a counterfeit. It is a tremendous thing to know one's assets, but just as tremendous to know one's liabilities or limitations — and Paul knew both. He talked about the Christian ministry as the real treasure of his life. In it he had "renounced the hidden things of dishonesty." He had neither walked in "craftiness" nor delivered the word of God "deceitfully." He had commended himself to every man's conscience through the "truth" in the sight of God. [4] Yet, honestly facing his limitations he added: "But we have this treasure in earthen vessels. . . ." [5] Again he wrote to the Christians at Corinth: "My inner self is perfectly known to God, and I hope, to your consciences too." [6] He was willing to expose the inner life. "In honor or dishonor, in slander or praise; considered a deceiver and yet true," [7] he struggled to keep his ministry free of inconsistency.

Everywhere the New Testament puts a premium on openness — being as one truly is. When Philip told Nathaniel that he had found the Messiah, Nathaniel retorted openly: "Can there any good thing come out of Nazareth?" Subsequently, Jesus met him and remarked: "Behold, an Israelite indeed, in whom is no guile." [8] There it is — "no guile," no deceit! Here was a man true to his impulsive nature, with whom there was no mask. This was the sort of man who at once won the heart of Christ.

[3] 1 Corinthians 9:27 (K.J.V.).
[4] 2 Corinthians 4:2 (K.J.V.).
[5] 2 Corinthians 4:7 (K.J.V.).
[6] 2 Corinthians 5:11 (C. B. Wms.).
[7] 2 Corinthians 6:8 (C. B. Wms.).
[8] See John 1:43-47 (K.J.V.).

Again, Matthew was one of the most despised citizens of Capernaum. He had sold his Jewish birthright into service of the Roman government as a tax collector to extort from his own people. Commonly called "publicans," the tax collectors were always numbered with the "sinners." Christ discovered Matthew and called him into His service. That might have been a time when Matthew would conceal his past for a more presentable appearance. But there was no attempt on his part to cover over his despicable character. Before he went away with Christ, he gave himself a going-away party — mainly because no one else would. But whom did he invite to the gathering? The other "publicans and sinners" along the seaboard! They were his drinking buddies who knew all about him. We might have acted a part by inviting the more reputable set for a better impression — but not Matthew. This is one of the reasons why Christ called him. He saw in Matthew a person who was the same on the inside as he was on the outside, and Christ could do something with a man who was "real."

Once Christ set a little child in the midst of the crowd who gathered, and said: "Of such is the kingdom of heaven." He was suggesting that those who would taste to the fullest what God has to offer men are those who would come as a little child. A child is innocent, open, teachable — the personification of candor. That is the attitude men were to adopt as the gateway to faith.

The fact that there was no civil war going on within Christ Himself is evidence that life was meant to be lived genuinely. He did not *feel* one way and *act* another. There was no difference between His sentiment and His expression. He walked into the sunlight for all to see, and men knew they were viewing the "real" Jesus, for they saw Him as He actually was. His inner life, rather than being wilfully covered up, arose spontaneously to the surface. As a result, He could walk erect. Being transparent He could live without the disabling fear of being found out.

This kind of genuineness gives to life its appropriate dignity. We need a kind of openness that will allow us to admit that which lurks in the shadows of our being. Admitting the true state of affairs is the only way to wholeness. There are times when I need to say: "Yes, I am lonely! Yes, I am rebellious! Sometimes I am discouraged and defeated! Undisciplined! Occasionally caustic and hardened! But I need your love — and perhaps you need mine!" When I can acknowledge my liabilities I become emotionally free from them. It is when I cannot face them that trouble comes. Freed to myself, I begin to express life without having to lower my head. That is dignity!

Legitimately, each of us is a role-player in life. For instance, I do not respond to my wife as I would to any of my friends, or to my best friend as I would to a total stranger. The roles we play are as varied as our relationships — yet without having to be false. The discrepancy comes when we assume these roles as if we were actors playing a part. I remember a girl who went from this country to England as a member of the cast for a traveling drama. After a month's tour she returned with a bogus English accent. (She was so jolly prim and proper that everyone took her for a bloody sight — and as quite unreal.)

The biblical description for this unrealistic staging is Christ's own riveting word — "hypocrite!" Of all people Christ most disliked the Pharisees because even in real life they were like "actors" playing a part. They wore the mask of the play, off stage as well as on. Their outward appearance, Christ said, was like whited gravestones, but inside they were filled with dead men's bones. They were like cups polished spotlessly on the outside but filled with pollution within. John the Baptist called them a "brood of vipers," quite descriptive of their fraudulent influence. The phrase was a parable on their hypocrisy because hypocrisy, like a *viper, poisons* the heart of the world. John's word of caution to them may be prophetic to our own lives: "Produce, then, fruit that is consistent with the repentance that you profess." [9]

Obviously the church cannot proceed on hypocrisy unless it chooses to leave an uncrossable gap between itself and the world. On the other hand, we must know what is meant by "openness of life" if we suggest its adoption in the church.

In one church I proposed a "round-table meeting" for each Sunday evening following the worship period. We would base the meeting on the New Testament term *sun-koinonia* (fellow-sharers) and our own need for dialogue on a personal level. We would not enter into a battle of wits to test one another's intellect. Neither would we uphold some religious system nor be concerned with theological or doctrinal issues. We would simply endeavor to share the experiences and meanings of our lives. We would implement prayer and waiting for guidance from the Spirit, and then everyone would be able to raise the questions that concerned him.

In my letter to the church I stressed that "openness of life" would characterize each meeting. We would throw the hidden cards of our lives onto the table unafraid to say what we honestly felt. Because we were all sinners and made mistakes, no one needed to feel a stranger. Because we had an understanding and forgiving God as a mutual trust, we could approach the meeting with assurance and acceptance which His grace affords.

To my chagrin, the proposal met with little response. Although I did not understand then why the suggestion was so unpromising, I can now appreciate the legitimate tension involved. Many had felt that "openness of life" meant "mutual confession of sins." [10] That seemed to be the going fad with some churches at the time — a "danger" that I had not anticipated.

What was misunderstood is that we can be "real" without

[9] Matthew 3:8 (C. B. Wms.).

[10] See Nat Tracy, "Venture into Spiritual Maturity," *Home Missions Magazine* of the Southern Baptist Convention (August, 1965), 10-12.

being interrogated; we can be "open" without being totally vulnerable. No one wants to go around displaying his wounded, ragged edges. What is unhealthy is for us to do or say that which is contrary to the welfare of our own conscience or to the conscience of others. Sometimes raw exposure of our inner life can become crude if not unnecessary.

Still, some have stressed that the normative community must be the *vulnerable community*. This is readily acceptable if what is meant is a candid exposure to the real Christian struggle rather than a mock demonstration of piety. We certainly must not make out as though we have no problems or as if we have all the answers. We must declare our "humanity" to the point of "risking" it with others. This will become at least an entrance for them. They can belong to that spirit and discover the hope we have without it sounding purely devotional. At all cost, we must not support unbridled vulnerability. We must not adopt an uncontrolled parade of our moral hang-ups. We may not be the *best* of specimens, but we need not be the *worst*. We may be transparent to God and man, genuine, honest, quick to offer testimony of our personal pilgrimage when it may be redemptive to human life.

The revelation of ourselves at the point of our strengths and weaknesses, the full-fledged entrance into the human race, and the dropping of our pseudo-sophistication, is more nearly what is meant by "openness of life." In the last analysis, we may not be able to define "openness" adequately, but we know when we have it and when we do not.

I was the pastor of another church for almost five years during which time I began to see the need for openness. During the last two years I attempted to promote it in the church. Many of the people had lived in the community all their lives and yet did not know the deep feelings of the persons in the pew next to them. The heartbeat of this church went out for "evangelism," while concern for the personal was only of remote interest.

A collection of positive and negative circumstances arose

in this church that eventually demanded my resignation. During the last few weeks of my tenure, some of us came to more openness with each other than during all those other years.

One man seeing my deep hurt over the decision to resign took me home with him. We went driving for a few hours and he helped me to get my bearings. Returning about eleven p.m., we pulled into the church yard and stopped. Then he said: "All right, I would like to hear again what you have been trying to do for at least the past two years in our church." For an hour I shared again my dream for the church. He listened and dialogued with me. This dialogue was a drama of what I had hoped for all along. Here were two men of the fellowship leveling with one another, revealing some deep feelings that had been bottled up too long.

In the same church I was able to open my life to another man as I pondered resignation. Although he was not a member of the church officially, he had become part of the "fellowship" — and I always treated him no less. He was a Christian and had been reared a Methodist. His wife was also a Christian but a Baptist. With mutual consent the entire family attended the Baptist church. Often someone would ask me: "Why don't you talk to him about becoming a Baptist?" My reply always was: "Why would I want to make a man of his convictions a Baptist, when as a Methodist he is already one of the finest Christian men in the community?" And he was. The demonstration of his life was proof enough.

Now, as I pondered resignation, I felt that he would understand me. I told him of my intentions to resign. (As I look back I see that my final decision to do so was not a mistake. The people needed some new blood in the pulpit. I had made some glaring blunders along the way, for which I still need their forgiveness. As much was wrong with me as with the church.)

A leading blunder that unsettled us as a fellowship was my preoccupation with one message. I was riding my dream —

a good horse no doubt — to death. Lack of diversity became boredom, and the church had a right to question my intent.

As I consulted my friend, his first appeal was that I wait a few months. Only a week passed, however, before I felt it best to resign. Standing in his yard one day I put to him my decision and he bade me Godspeed with tears in his eyes. Although things had not turned out the way either of us might have liked, this experience brought us to an openness with each other that helped to heal my life during those difficult days. Someone knew the real me deep down!

In conclusion, how may we begin our quest for openness in the church? The following steps may be of practical help.

1. *The first step is to go through the discerning acid test of self-honesty.* I must look inward and admit the true state of affairs. When I have done something unreal or underhanded, I must be willing to look into the mirror of my conscience. It is not helpful to dodge the issue by simply saying, "The Devil made me do it!"

2. *Second, I must realize that however sordid the results of my self-analysis, my case is not hopeless.* I must not sit in judgment upon myself. I must accept who I am knowing that I have Christ's guarantee that the true state of affairs does not draw God's wrath. Honesty is my only hope for spiritual life and renewal; therefore, I can commit my inner life to Jesus Christ without fear.

3. *When I discover pretense in my life I must combat it rather than dress it up.*

One way to combat it is to repent for being the kind of person who has to cover up. That is quite practical because I am forced to discern the *reason* for my hiding. Then I can meet the *conditions* of repentance by blasting loose the blockage.

There is another way to combat pretense. When I have lied, or presumed to be something that I am not (such as trying to impress others when I am not very impressive), then I can teach my heart a lesson by kindly asking forgiveness of those with whom I failed to be genuine. A few occasions like this will produce in me a sensitivity toward integrity.

4. *A fourth step is to find one other person with whom I can share all if I feel the need.* I can find acceptance and support only as I reveal my inward, unseen life to another — "for what person knows a man's thoughts except the spirit of the man which is in him?" [11] The reason Christ could call His disciples "friends" instead of "servants" at the end of His ministry was that, as He put it: "I have told you everything that I have learned from my Father." [12] He had revealed all.

5. When I have tasted openness with one other person, *the next step is to find a small group in the Christian community who will accept me unconditionally.* As I feel free to share my thoughts, my struggles and my aspirations without being criticized, then I am secure enough to be more liberated at large. I must first have openness among those who accept me so the pain of publicly bringing down the mask will not be unbearable. The reality in my life then is not so raw that I must cloak it from society. Conversely, without this "fellowship," openness ends in despair.

6. *A sixth step is to test my openness to others.* The refined sentiment of love spontaneously called forth will become that test. Love must be unshakable. When nothing can drive it away I know that I am open. When men can see my utter concern for their welfare, their problems, their dreams, at any cost to myself, they will no longer be looking at a person who has closed his life to them — and that kind of person will serve as a bridge between the church and the world.

7. In the final analysis, by no means the least step,

11 1 Corinthians 2:11 (r.s.v.).
12 John 15:15 (C. B. Wms.).

I must come to God with my unreality. I must remember with Job that "with him is strength: the deceived and the deceiver are his." [13]

To discover that we are desperately self-deceptive beings and often insensitive to everyone around us is a remarkable unveiling. The discovery is made best in a community of unmasked persons where openness exists as the first step toward reality and maturity. Consequently, the bridge of self-exposure is the gateway to fellowship, both for the church and for the world.

[13] Job 12:16 (K.J.V.).

Chapter 4

A Versatile Form

> Come, now, suppose there
> were no churches, no chapels,
> no sermons, no assemblies for
> worship, wouldst thou still be
> a Christian?
>
> — *C. H. Spurgeon*

Everyone has something rich to give out of his inner life
and character. Were this not true, the early Christian community would have been severely handicapped, for it had no
organization or property to offer the world.

The only "property" possessed by the early Christian
community was its own character and life gained through
its relationship with Jesus Christ. In a real sense it possessed nothing — yet was steward of everything. On the one
hand, it surrendered its material effects to Rome under fire,
while on the other hand, it abdicated the citadel of its inner
life to Jesus Christ. Yet this intangible ingredient became
its wealth, for Rome could not confiscate this "inheritance
of the saints." What the writer of Hebrews wrote the second
generation Christians in A.D. 65 is explanatory:

> Be ever mindful of the days gone by in which, after
> you were first spiritually enlightened, you endured a
> great and painful struggle, sometimes being yourselves
> a gazingstock, publicly exposed to insults and abuse and
> distress, and sometimes claiming fellowship and making

common cause with others who were so treated. For you did sympathize and suffer along with those who were imprisoned, and you bore cheerfully the plundering of your belongings and the confiscation of your property, in the knowledge and consciousness that you yourselves had a better and lasting possession. [1]

Rome might have been doing Christianity a favor in pressing the community inward to a basic solidarity with itself. Now the community had to minister strictly out of its inner life. The Faith was forced back upon sole dependence in the resources of Jesus Christ; for Rome certainly offered none. Religion had to be life or nothing. Christianity was not to be entered lightly. To make it one's supreme value became costly; for the imperial cult was after blood – Christian blood. This was proof in itself that the early community, like a living tree, was *vascular,* not *institutional.* Cut into its heart and it would bleed, not crumble.

There is nothing nostalgic in the modern church for this way of living. We can sympathize but we cannot know the full impact of the Roman persecution. There was something magificently winsome and transforming about a people struggling at such odds. In reality there was more beauty in fisher folk and market men, when they were precisely Christian, than in the legates of the Empire. They lacked institutional power, were unrecognized by the state, and were largely uneducated. Still, an inner strength broke brighter upon the ancient horizon in the people of God than shone in the strong-arm tactics of Caesarism. A dying people made an undying impact upon the world.

Under such travail one wonders how Christianity survived. There were no church buildings with stained glass windows, no cathedrals of comfort, no parochial centers of worship. Such lack, however, did not impede the Christian movement. As a sect within Judaism itself, its only material domain had been an early association with the local synagogues and the Temple in Jerusalem. However, when the Christian

[1] Hebrews 10:32-34 *(The Amplified New Testament).*

adherents were forced out of the Jewish synagogue, they went next door with their true "possession" and set up house-keeping in private homes. From this point, the church could rightly be called the "house-church community."

The Book of Acts relates what generally took place when believers met together in the home. They studied the apostles' teaching, shared in fellowship, broke bread together and prayed. [2] Such courage was generated in these meetings that when Peter and the other apostles were seized by the Sanhedrin, warned in their valor against preaching in the name of Christ, and then set free, the Book of Acts begins to read like a chivalrous novel: "Not for a single day did they stop teaching in the temple square and in private houses the good news of Jesus the Christ." [3] Whatever went on behind closed doors became explosive in the open.

For this reason the early form intrigues us. We are moved by the fact that hundreds of small societies met in such homes as those of Aquila and Priscilla, Philemon, and Nympha for precisely spiritual reasons. [4] Each had a peculiar impact upon its contemporaries. From these we easily gather why Paul described the Christian community as the "family of God" and as the "household of faith." [5] Here was a closely knit unit whose interests and dreams seemed to be going in a mutual direction. Like the family, its intimacy established a sense of security and dependency. This, in turn, gave courage for venturing into the world. Moreover, being known and loved of a "heavenly Father" made it possible for the "household" to accept and cherish one another unconditionally.

Whether we look to the church or to the home, these tremendous expressions of life seem largely novel to us today. However, the modern trend is a longing for such a "place."

In our study groups some persons have asked why the

[2] Acts 2:42.
[3] Acts 5:42 (C. B. Wms.).
[4] See Romans 16:5; 1 Corinthians 16:19; Colossians 4:15; Philemon 2.
[5] Ephesians 2:21; Galatians 6:10.

church chose the home if it was not the most likely "place" for Christianity to develop. If it worked for Proconsular Asia why wouldn't it work for America? Should it not also become the modern style?

Speaking to the first issue, we must show the unimpeachable reasons for the early "home" style. Monumental splendor and material abundance marked the Roman age, but the church was not at liberty to share in this opulance. The early church met in homes for one reason only: their circumstance was one of *privation*. (Remember, Rome had confiscated all Christian property except for private houses, and Judaism had pushed them from the synagogues into the streets.) There is nothing ingenuous about privation — the church would not have chosen it. There was simply no other place to meet, except in houses, in caves, or in some instances under the guise of the trade guilds in the Catacombs. (It is almost ironic to add that under the guise of the funeral guilds Christianity rather than *burying* was *bringing to life* — spiritual life.)

Speaking to the second issue, we must not preclude the possibility that the modern church, as to form, must meet in homes, because the church in our day is neither as indigent nor as exposed as was the church in the early Christian era. However, we must be careful that we do not impose upon everyone the institutional church's demand for a building. Some meeting place is necessary, obviously, or we discredit the New Testament idea of the "gathered church." We must fear, however, lest that place becomes our moral death. As Winston Churchill put it: "We shape our dwellings, and afterward our dwellings shape us."

The *needs of the fellowship* should always dictate to the *formation* of the church and not the other way around. Because this is true, the formative principle for the church in any age is *versatility*. The early church was not without its form. No church is. Yet, it did not become rigid or indispensably conventional. It organized according to its circumstances. The home design may have been most conducive to its own spirit of openness, but such form had to remain malleable; for each successive age has conditioning all its own. The house-church principle does, however, warrant that the modern church — wherever its meeting place — must be concerned chiefly with its life and spirit rather than with its locality and building complex on the street corner.

Concern over concrete, brick, and asphalt tends to "localize" the spirit of God's people to damaging degrees. Christianity becomes easily equated with "Church Street Assembly" about eleven o'clock each Sunday morning and other prevailing times thereafter. To show the irony, a few years ago one pastor reprimanded a group of young people among his membership because rather than coming to services *at their own church* they were sharing their testimonies in other churches. Here they were *ministering to people* every Sunday by invitation, being and living what Christianity is all about, and their own pastor could not support them.

Many times those who are not found "going" to church regularly are regarded by those who do go as either nominal Christians or not Christians at all. I am aware that the writer of Hebrews exhorts us not to forsake the assembling of ourselves together, but the issue is "where." Many deeply concerned Christians are finding the conventional worship services spiritually defeating rather than enlivening. For some, the real meeting between persons, the valuable encounter, and the transforming power which come from open intimate dialogue in depth, all hold precedence.

What could be wrong? The present form and procedure may not be in step with the present spirit. As a result, small groups are springing up everywhere, either in lieu of the church meetings or in addition to them. A great number of people have found creative living more readily in the casual home-style settings as over against the more traditional mass meetings of the cathedral and church establishments. For these, the modern church is undergoing a change into smaller units — encounter groups, study groups, prayer groups, and fellowship groups. These extra-ecclesiastical communities, or *koinonia* groups, are appearing with the hope of promising the needed boon.

A tide of these *koinonia* groups is pressing the institutional shores. Centers of renewal, retreat lodges, coffee houses, counseling centers and various other innovative ministries are gearing themselves for the new breed of people seeking a "place." These emerging centers are often renounced by the institutional church as daring to assume the role of the church. Those offering the criticism tend to have forgotten that the church is the "people of God" — wherever they express themselves. The assumption of these centers may therefore be observed either as a *legitimate desire* for a life-producing community of faith or as a *potential threat* to the established church as it presently stands.

If the upsurge of the small group movement is not enough to awaken the modern church to the role of creating a vital community, then it is no fault of the thousands hungering for reality if they appear to be somewhat "unorthodox." The cry now is that the church at least make "community" a matter of desperate concern. Maybe we feel that men should help produce community within the already-existing structure. The only demand, of course, is that the concern be there in one form or another. J. C. Hoekendijk goes so far as to add: "It may be necessary to create them (extra-church communities) as an interim measure. But we should realize that as soon as these halfway communities between church and world become a permanent feature, we have in fact given up hope for the church." [6]

A number of alternatives today are vying for prominence. The following list may show how varied the difference of opinion really is:

  1. Many people are completely satisfied with the church as it presently stands.
  2. Some established churches have sometimes re-

[6] J. C. Hoekendijk, *The Church Inside Out*, ed. by L. A. Hoedemaker and Pieter Tijmes; trans. by Isaac C. Rottenberg (Philadelphia: The Westminster Press, 1966), p. 29. Parenthesis are mine.

belled when the demand for change has been too sudden. At other times it has welcomed *koinonia* groups as an adjunct to the present church order.

3. The so-called "underground church" as a modern movement has tried to exercise openness of life, while eliminating the modern church form altogether.

4. Still others are attempting to renew the church to its vital aspect, while trying to salvage the present order.

In all this, two *extremes* are beginning to emerge.

On the one hand, some exponents of "church renewal" have largely said "no" to the present form of the church and have gone back to reclaim the house-church setting. This particular camp of the renewal movement has withdrawn into a damaging extreme, not in that it has desired the more intimate, dialogical approach to religion, but in that it has tended to *interrupt the valuable complex of home life.*

A number of us pursued such a venture for one year. We discovered — at least in our attempt at renewal — that the home is no ideal center for the trafficking of "church" at all hours. We found that the nature of the church as a total living together for lengthy intervals, militated against the health of both home and church. Occasional prayer meetings, Bible studies, sharing conferences, and other similar gatherings in the home seemed altogether valid. As for any prolonged extension of those meetings, we discovered it to be a practical imposition. We concluded that the household flourished far better as a home than as a church.

We had mistakenly identified the New Testament *norm* of the church with its *form.* We felt that the home style was necessary before real sharing and openness could be maintained. Informality had given us much more hope in this direction, but we soon learned that this normative quality depended solely upon the *people* and not upon the *place.* Perhaps there is some educational significance in the name we selected — "*Laos*" (people) rather than "*Topos*" (place).

We almost fell again into the vicious circle of making the "church" the "holy place of God" instead of the "holy people of God."

For reasons unlike those of the early Christian era, the homes of our era, we soon realized, need to maintain a stronghold of privacy. The early Christians retreated to the homes because the *tension* was in the *world*. We must go elsewhere because our *tension* is in the *home*. The chief frontier for Christian wholeness today is family life. It is not the place for corporate Christian retreat; it is the place for individual Christian renewal.

At the same time, it occurred to us that the center of meeting need not be the stereotyped, pew-filled convening center where monologue thrives. It might in fact be the more casual, simplified atmosphere of a "fellowship house" separate from the home. We have since learned that here, more than any other place, the church can be the normative community without disrupting home life while helping to redeem it.

Even if the trend now is away from Gothic architecture toward the more elemental "meeting-house" idea, it seems altogether fitting that the institutional church (if it can minimize the phony sacredness of facility) may well serve as such a "meeting-house." Only as it recaptures the normative principle of "openness of life" can it do so. There seems to be no valid reason, otherwise, for the modern extremity of adopting the New Testament form. As Charles Jefferson put it: "Informality is not evidence of piety nor a scorn of forms proof of exalted spirituality." [7]

There is a second extreme which has to do with the *traditional* Christian form of the church. The institutional church has so "canonized" its present *form* that now we have to struggle against a "forced image" — with little hope of anything different. This insight comes from Hoekendijk who writes: "From an incidental pattern it became a normative

[7] Charles E. Jefferson, *The Building of the Church* (New York: The Macmillan Company, 1913), p. 128.

model; from a historically conditioned phenomenon it became an unchangeable divine institution." [8] Whether we like it or not, Protestantism has thus retained a "structural pope" to which many give allegiance consciously or unconsciously. With many, the *building* has become the supreme Christian symbol. To admit the falseness of this extremity to ourselves may not help our Protestant affirmation, but it may help our Christianity.

Presently, we are having to live with this imposed model to such extent that some people, quite unconsciously, have equated being Christian with regular attendance in this arbitrarily established structure. In his Confessions, Augustine recorded a conversation between Victorinus and Simplicianus which humorously depicts this misleading view of the relationship between Christianity and the church. When Simplicianus remarked that he could not believe that Victorinus had become a Christian until he saw him attending the church, Victorinus questioned: "Is it then the walls that make Christians?" [9] Similarly, the renowned nineteenth century preacher of the Metropolitan Tabernacle in London, Charles Haddon Spurgeon, once put the proposition to his parish flock: "Come, now, suppose there were no churches, no chapels, no sermons, no assemblies for worship, wouldst thou still be a Christian?" [10]

Buildings may be a sign that *people want roots,* but no one can *belong* to a building. Bricks should never have become sacred, for mortar has never welded together the human spirit into unity and love. If some persons do not find roots of warmth and adventure in the modern church procedure, it is due to the *spirit* within the walls and not the *material mold* itself. Erecting buildings to God, therefore, is neither sinful nor destructive. They may become

[8] Hoekendijk, *Op. Cit.,* p. 98.

[9] *The Confessions of Augustine,* trans. by J. G. Pilkington (by permission of Liveright Publishing Corp., © 1943), p. 165.

[10] C. H. Spurgeon, "Life's Ever-Springing Well," *The Metropolitan Tabernacle Pulpit,* Vol. XV, p. 198.

great assets or great deficits, depending on the spirit of God's people.

The lesson to be learned here is that God does His redemptive work at the citadel of the heart, and therefore He must not be bound within the fabrication of walls in the people's minds. In one chapter of Isaiah, the Lord may be paraphrased as saying: "The thing that interests me is not your houses, for what house can you build for me? What interests me is the open, contrite spirit and reverence for my word. . . . But I have called and no one has answered, and I have spoken but no one has listened." [11] Not to be open to God is the first indication that, for all our architectural comfort, only the shell of religion stands. Any kind of belonging within that shell is purely accidental.

Thus we see the dangers inherent within these two extremes — the disrupting of home life on the one hand and preoccupation with an imposed model on the other.

What may be the corrective for these two extremes? It may not be simply a happy medium between the two that will satisfy the longing for Christian excellence — but somewhere along the line between the two every Christian community should be able to find the form compatible with its own spiritual outlook. The guiding principle for preserving the versatility and appropriateness of the form must include at least the following elements:

1. The *spirit* must take precedence over the structure.
2. The Christian Community must remain open and sensitive to the Spirit of God.
3. The procedure must comply with current need.

The relation between the *spirit* and *structure* of religion has always been a problem in history. This is especially true in the history of Israel. At one point, David "prayed that he might be allowed to find a dwelling place for the God of Jacob." [12] God quickly showed him that the dwelling

[11] Isaiah 66:1-4 (Paraphrase).
[12] Acts 7:46 (Amplified).

place He intended was not a physical structure but a people in whom He could reside. [13] He had already symbolized His universal presence among His people by sanctioning the Tabernacle as a mobile unit. A stabilized center of worship might even curtail the spirit of religion into merely symbolizing national pride. The pagan religions had already "localized" their gods by building monuments to them. There was this same pagan danger for Israel. This must not be allowed, because "God is a Spirit: and they that worship him must worship him in spirit and in truth."[14] Under David, "a man after God's own heart," it was not permitted, but under Solomon whose wisdom prevailed over God's intention, it was. [15] When Solomon completed his building, he exclaimed woefully: "Behold heaven and the highest heaven cannot contain thee; how much less this house which I have built!" [16] Soul-sickness always follows one's attempt to confine God.

In the New Testament we discover that the first great controversy between Judaism and Christianity concerned Israel's preoccupation with confining God to the Temple and her failure to be open to Him.

Speaking to the first issue, for Christianity the "temple" referred to God's people, and for Judaism, it was the sacred building in Jerusalem. In the years to follow, the Christian church would not adopt the traditional procedure. Whatever form it assumed, it would revive the highly expressive meaning of God's presence which the Temple was meant to symbolize. Later, Paul actually referred to the church as the "temple of God." [17] He spoke metaphorically of *the people in whom Christ dwelt* — the fulfillment of David's dream. In his second letter to the Corinthian community

[13] See 2 Samuel 7:8-29; Psalm 132.

[14] John 4:24 (k.j.v.).

[15] See Acts 7:47; 1 Kings 6. Note in verses 12-13 that God accommodated Himself to Solomon's desire but on the condition that it would not destroy the spirit of obeying His will. The promise made to David would be extended to Solomon and God would again dwell among His people.

[16] 2 Chronicles 6:18 (r.s.v.).

[17] 1 Corinthians 3:16, 17.

Paul wrote: "For, as for us, we are an *inner sanctuary* of the living God, even as God said, I will dwell in them in fellowship with them as in a home and I will live my life in and through them. And I will be their God and they themselves will be my people." [18]

The second issue has to do with openness to God. Stephen began the controversy by confronting the Jewish Sanhedrin with the closed-minded hearing that had prevailed among Judaism throughout its entire history. He called for renewal within institutionalized Judaism much the same as reformers today are calling for renewal of institutionalized Christianity. He first told the Pharisees that "the most High does not dwell in houses and temples made with hands." [19] Then he added the striking statement familiar from many of the ancient prophets: "You stiff-necked people, uncircumcised in heart and ears, you always resist the Holy Spirit." [20] Here again is the tension between being open to the Spirit and being bound by the structure, the battle between the norm and the form.

When Stephen reminded the Pharisees of the "sacred compact of circumcision" once made to Abraham, he put his finger on the most crucial problem of God's people for all ages — the problem of the *insensitive heart.* Circumcision had become the physical sign of the Covenant offered unconditionally to Israel. It symbolized the open-hearted posture of God's people toward that Covenant and toward the God of that Covenant. What could the call of the Deuteronomist mean — "Circumcise therefore the foreskin of your heart, and be no longer stubborn" [21] — unless it was the call to cut away the insulation of the heart so that the warmth and love of God could get in? Circumcision, in this instance, could only mean a heart made pliable and sensitive

[18] 2 Corinthians 6:16 (*Wuest's Translation,* Kenneth S. Wuest. Wm. B. Eerdmans Publishing Co. Used by permission.) Italics are mine.

[19] Acts 7:48 (Amplified).

[20] Acts 7:51 (R.S.V.).

[21] Deuteronomy 10:16 (R.S.V.).

to the will and purpose of God. Knowing this, Paul could later write to the Christians at Rome: "Real circumcision is heart-circumcision, a spiritual, not a literal affair." [22] To the Philippian church he announced: "For we are the true circumcision, who worship God in spirit, and glory in Christ Jesus, and put no confidence in the flesh." [23]

Whether in confining God to a structure or in failing to be open to Him we are very capable of putting Christianity into some sacred rut. To remain spiritually alive, we must always be bursting out of those formations of the church which are no longer relevant to the human spirit. No one will long endure a procedure that does not comply with current need.

The form is important but not so important that we substitute mere colorful bricks for our colorless lives.

[22] Romans 2:29 (C. B. Wms.).
[23] Philippians 3:3 (R.S.V.).

Chapter 5

The Centered-power of Community

> It is not civilization and cul-
> ture, nor blood and soil, that
> can really unite us but only
> love, disinterested, sacrificing,
> selfless love — that love which
> Jesus Christ alone gives us.
>
> — *Emil Brunner*

The early church was a fellowship of people bonded not by occasional and superficial contacts but on a life together in all its common ventures. It was capable of withstanding the external threat of martyrdom, but sometimes it buckled under the shapeless edges of its own "humanity." Certainly it exhibited flaws and made mistakes! Every group, however Christianized, proceeds upon a pilgrimage from which the human element cannot be removed.

Struggle and apparent failure make threatening inroads into every church because the raw edges of our humanity outrage the elements of imperfect-faith and imperfect-love within the life of the community. In spite of our frailty, however, there is hope for growing unity and strength if the early Christian community is any substantial model. In the face of its troubles *something overpowering cemented the church's life and brought success of purpose to bear.*

The life of Jesus Christ in the midst of community became the cement that welded together the elite and the common, the nameless and the aristocrat, the Jew and the Greek, the bond and the free. There could not have been the uniting of such divergent elements without His transforming love. Such love became the *centered-power of community*. Amazingly, it was able to drive men toward unity within, and to increase life and preserve its power of redemptiveness to the outside world.

Emil Brunner pointedly reminds us that "it is not civilization and culture, nor blood and soil, that can really unite us but only love, disinterested, sacrificing, selfless love — that love which Jesus Christ alone gives us." [1]

Looking back to the first few centuries A.D., we can understand why the world was affected so deeply by Christianity. The early community had an approachable quality stemming from its ability to love. It did not resort to *total withdrawal* as did the church of the Reformation and thereby raise the world's pride. Nor did it resort to *enforcement* as did the church of the Counter-Reformation and thereby raise the world's anger and fear. Nor did it resort to an *empty success-image* as in the Post-Reformation period and thereby raise the world's indifference, where we stand today.

The early community had a different attitude. The worst and the best were compelled by its servant-love. Not all but most recognized the magnitude of such a vital minority. Here was a people who could out-do, out-live, out-give, out-love, out-wait, out-suffer, out-laugh, out-cry, any other people. In a short time, power groups and individuals were weakening to the spreading winsomeness of this servant-love, sanctioned for its reality and power in life. Even the virile Roman ship of state was being capsized by the potency of Christian unity and love. On one occasion the Jewish leaders of Thessalonica rushed to the City Council with the urgent warning: "These who turned the Roman empire up-

1 Emil Brunner, *I Believe in the Living God,* trans. and edited by John Holden (Philadelphia, Pa.: The Westminster Press, 1961), p. 136.

side down, have arrived here also." [2] The reality of the Christian life came across either as a promise or as a plague to move men. Such centered-power bred response or resistance but never indifference.

What elements composed such a dynamic that the entire course of history was changed in just a few brief years? How could Christianity in twenty-five years from its inception spread from Palestine, to Rome? What made the relationship within the community so responsive to one another and to the living Christ, and the relationship outside the community so responsible?

The community had a *circumference* and a *center*. In these two essentials lay the human and divine source of its potency.

The circumference consisted of a band of ordinary people united on common ground, out of a common need, for projecting a common aim. A very natural, human form of love engrossed them — it was simply the love of human affiliation, the longing for affinity with one another.

In the New Testament this love is referred to as *philia* from the verb root *phileo*. We often use this Greek root today without being aware of it. For instance, we talk of *Philadelphia* without knowing that it means "brotherly love," hence a "friendly city." We use *philanthropist* unaware of its meaning — "lover of man" or "friend of man." Whereas *phileo* means "to be friendly toward" or "to delight in," most biblical versions translate it as "to love."

To be a lover, in so far as *philia* is concerned, is to be a *friend* — and all men need to be that. Friendships are formed on man's common need to be accepted and cherished, or on elements of affinity in each other to which one is drawn. Common to each of us is the need to belong. Inherent in every man is an ego-bias that demands attention. We can easily see why this kind of love became the starting place for the Christian community.

Philia, however, is not strong enough to hold us together.

[2] Acts 17:6 (Wuest).

The early church would have died had it not gone beyond this quality of love. It is easy to see why when we note the self-centered nature of this love. It is a love that leans more strongly toward one's own personal ends than toward those who are loved. A mercenary quality of getting returns predominates it. Whether we like it or not, most of us proceed on this quality of love — demanding ounce for ounce, tit for tat. This attitude "delights in" relationships for what it may receive from them. Although it bears certain mutual qualities, it is basically self-oriented. It is no wonder then that our world gives place to "broken relationships."

Psychology uses the term *philia* to describe the basic family relationship. As I have wondered why, I have concluded that it is because this love projects a possessive quality based largely on self-absorbing emotions. It really does describe the family, for *we are a people of attachment.* This love shows itself when a son goes off to college, or when a daughter marries, or when a relative dies. We see how possessive we have been, how protective, how attached — how self-centered. Parents who possess or over-protect their children do it under the guise of love — inferior love, of course, because it does not take to heart the freedom and strength necessary for their children's fulfillment.

Here is a girl who sits in my office unburdening her dismal plight in life because she never knew what real love is. She had only known a possessive, overbearing sort of attachment. Both parents were extremely domineering. She was never allowed to handle her own affairs. Even the slightest freedom to purchase her own clothing was denied her. An adequate understanding of her own sexuality had been frustrated because of this dominance. She never had enduring relationships with her friends because no matter how appropriately she invited them into the home she would always — as she put it — "catch it" from her father. Now that she is much older she is like a helmless vessel. She cannot fit into the real world of other people because her early life has left her without an adequate personal foundation. Now she has grown rebellious. Resentment has turned to hatred, hatred to guilt feelings, guilt feelings to frustration, and frustration to despair. In eight years she has gone through five psychiatrists and currently floats adrift in a heartless sea of drugs and alcohol.

What went wrong? Her parents loved her for themselves, and because they did, they have lost her and have become lost to themselves in the process. Could they not have "delighted in" the relationship without perverting it? Yet, how easily perversion comes.

I want to come back now and apply this analogy to the church because the church became an "intimate circle" on the basis of this love. This kind of love, because it was tinted with aspects of self-centeredness, defined the circumference and the limit of relationship. At first the believers were the circumference; they were the limit! This was partly due to the fact that persecution had pushed them underground for awhile — but it was also due to the basically self-centered drives coherent within the community. *They* met to worship the living God and the Christ who made Him so vividly real. *They* supported one another for daily pilgrimage into their homes, their jobs, and their relationships. *They* faced and resolved personal conflicts. All the present challenges of the day were ignited by *their* having been together in the name of Christ.

What kept the community then from cultivating an eccentric mode of existence? What kept it from becoming a prideful perimeter, ingrown and exclusive? What kept it from becoming totally self-centered, concerned chiefly with its own welfare?

The Christian community had a *center* — a center that became its power. That center was the *God-kind of love (agape)* infused into the fellowship by the living Christ. The following is a general characterization of this divine love.

    1. *Unrequited.* It receives us where we are, requiring nothing in return.

2. *Unconditional.* It accepts and forgives us on the basis of God's character and not on the basis of our own. There are no conditions that we must meet in order for God to love us; we could never merit it.

3. *Vicarious.* It takes our place by paying the death penalty for our rebellion, assuming both the responsibility and cure of our sinful nature.

4. *Other-centered.* It reaches out for what is best in the one loved, laboring to fulfill the persons on whom Christ set His affection.

5. *Servant-love.* It reaches its peak in self-giving, bearing the spirit of the Suffering Servant (Christ) who serves out of a combined sense of dignity and humility.

6. *Righteous-love.* It bears a rugged quality that demands justice, allowing man neither to violate his own nature nor the nature of God without serious consequence to himself.

7. *Compassionate.* It is longsuffering, keeping mercy for all and making a way for cleansing men of guilt.

If we could share in this divine love it would emit a power that would coalesce us as the people of God. We would make an impact upon life. However, if God's purpose is to have the effect upon the world that it deserves, His love must not be misconstrued. Sometimes we have cheapened or weakened God's love by our mistaken concepts of it. Let me take three of the above characteristics, for instance, and show how we can fall into an improper shading of them.

First, whereas God's love is unconditional some have thought of it as *bribing* instead. They have said that God sent His Son to bribe us into loving and serving Him. This is seen all too well in our theologically mistaken Christian hymn which says: "I gave my life for thee; what hast thou given for me?"

To attribute this attitude to God does violence both to His character and to man's. He becomes a coercive God who demands love in return. He loves not because it is His nature to love but in order to get love. This makes Him a selfish Being. This love also violates man because it makes him a robot to be manipulated and preys on his sense of guilt to get a response rather than eliciting a response on the basis of love.

The truth is that God offers love unconditionally. Whether we respond or not does not affect His love. He goes on loving in spite of us. Neither must we ask God to love us; it is His nature to do so. We do not have to go into our yard each morning and say to the sun, "Shine!" It is the nature of the sun to shine; it does not ask us to meet certain conditions before it will. Neither does God.

In the second place, *God's love is tough — not indulgent.* We have not grasped the true nature of God if we have thought Him to be either a nightstick-wielding celestial policeman or an indulgent grandfather who never vents His anger. His love is nonetheless strong. He must be both a God of love and a God of wrath, and the two qualities are not contradictory. God's wrath is the justice side of His love without which love is purely indulgent. He is a God who must bring justice to bear or He is not moral, a God who must show love or He is not merciful.

Man certainly needs mercy but he needs correction and discipline, too, for his own fulfillment. Indulgence leaves us spoiled if not totally self-centered — yet, "Do as you please!" is the cry of our permissive age. The old adage remains true even for our undisciplined culture — "Spare the rod and spoil the child." The ancient proverb is stronger still: "He who spares the rod hates his son, but he who loves him is diligent to discipline him." [3]

God is producing honorable sons, not illegitimate children. He is offering humanity a kind of sonship that bears the essence of the Father. That essence cannot come through cheap grace or flippancy. The writer of Hebrews asks:

[3] Proverbs 13:24 (r.s.v.).

Have you fogotten the exhortation which addresses you
as sons? —

> "My son, do not regard lightly the discipline of the
>   Lord,
> nor lose courage when you are punished by him.
> For the Lord disciplines him whom he loves, and
> chastises every son whom he receives."

It is for discipline that you have to endure. God is treat-
ing you as sons; for what son is there whom his father
does not discipline? If you are left without discipline, in
which all have participated, then you are illegitimate
children and not sons. [4]

The writer goes on to conclude that God disciplines us
for our own good, that we may share in His holiness. If
God is merely indulgent then He does not care about our
wholeness. We are thus surrendered to self-destruction.

Another way of expressing the strength of God's love is
that it is tough-skinned and tough-hearted. *Agape* may sometimes find it difficult to get up once it has been knocked
down, but if it is *Love*, it will sooner or later get up, and
then it will come back to the source of conflict without resentment. A God who will not run away from me when I
spurn Him is a God who eventually overpowers my heart.

On the other hand, He is tough-hearted because He intends my wholeness. Tough-heartedness in this sense is not
personal defiance; it is restorative.

A few years ago I was invited to a home gathering in
Fort Worth, Texas to hear Gert Behanna (author of *The
Late Liz*). As she shared her understanding of Christian love
I exploded emotionally within. Luckily, I captured verba-
tim one small fragment of her witness, even to the punctua-
tion that pierced my ears. She said: "Love is tough. You
better believe it! Sometimes it has to 'take it'; sometimes it
has to 'give it.' And of course the greatest love is a man
hanging on a cross with nails in Him — and if you think
that isn't tough, maybe you would like to try it."

[4] Hebrews 12:5-8 (R.S.V.).

Third, the God-kind of love bears *a remarkable compassion — not pity*. There is certainly a difference between the two. Pity is a sympathetic sorrow for distress, whereas compassion is an awareness of distress with a desire to alleviate it. Pity stands at arms length; compassion draws near. The New Testament declares that when Christ saw the people like sheep having no shepherd He had *compassion* on them. That compassion ended in reaching out to them — loving them, not pitying them.

There is something in us that is repulsed by attitudes of pity. When Christ was walking down the Via Dolorosa on His way to die, the women who followed Him pitifully lamented His death. That pity was a degrading response, like that described by the poet Cather: "pity . . . that was for the murderer on the scaffold, as it was for the dying soldier or the martyr on the rack." This whimpering of defeat repulsed Christ; He was not a victim but a Victor. No man took His life from Him. He laid it down of His own accord and had the power to take it up again. He turned to the women and said, "Daughters of Jerusalem, do not weep for me, but weep for yourselves and for your children." [5] Whatever else the dying love of Christ should elicit from the heart of man, it should elicit love and not pity.

In 1965, I read a very moving story about a disaster that happened to the village of Humlikon, Switzerland. On September 4, 1963, forty-three farm people from Humlikon boarded a plane along with thirty-seven others for a one-day excursion to Geneva. Their purpose was to inspect a fertilizer plant there. Enroute the plane crashed, killing all on board. A whole generation of Humlikon's people was instantly wiped out. Generous concern came immediately from the outside world to those families left desolate. People came to tend the farms, milk the cows, feed the chickens, and to care for the orphaned children. Many offered labor and sent money. Gifts poured in amounting to $350,000.

[5] Luke 23:28 (r.s.v.).

The first Christmas following the crash, and every Christmas thereafter, gifts and toys were made available to the children of Humlikon. On one particular Christmas when the gifts came pouring in, one teenage girl expressed her hurt.

> She bent her head in embarrassed silence.
> Finally she said, "Please understand. We are very thankful. To everybody. But" — her voice became a strained whisper — "our mama and papa gave us presents because they loved us. Strangers send presents because they pity us. It hurts always to be pitied." [6]

There is a desperation in man to grasp the love that will fill the vacuum of the heart. There is, at the same time, an awesome fear that when it is offered to him in Christ, it will demand the whole extremity of his life. It is costly because it places man under a new bondage. It makes demands on his total being. A love like this is difficult to assimilate precisely because the self-absorbing nature of man insulates rather than opens itself to it. When God's love draws near, it is rarely accepted without a struggle. This love is a conquest greatly feared, for it threatens to take away the sovereignty of one's life.

The promising value of choosing this kind of love, rather than shunning it, is that when it is infused into the Christian community, it penetrates the circumference, breaks down the limits the group has established for itself, without destroying them, and turns the members to a world-wide concern. This love gives a new motivation for living redemptively. Moreover, it gives a formidable courage that the community did not have before.

When Christian communities have been built on *philia* alone, the outcome has generally been one of futility, lacking depth and reality. Unity becomes short-lived, and concern for the world becomes a superficial claim. Proceeding without an abandonment to the God-kind of love, these communities somehow have a tendency instead to *unite them-*

[6] Oscar Schisgall, "The Village Where People Cared." *Reader's Digest* (February, 1965), LXXXVI:60.

selves against the outside world as a different breed of humanity. This happens because they allow themselves to become pridefully isolated, consciously or unconsciously. The expression of the church then becomes one of ethical platitudes and moralism to the world at large rather than one bearing a spirit of servanthood. At the same time, the lack of *agape* eventually leaves the community within in disharmony and disarray simply because *philia* alone cannot exclude the struggles for power within the group. It enhances rather than alters the ego, the self-centered drives of the human heart.

Only the commitment of God's people to the God-kind of love can preserve it as a centered-power — for only *agape* has the germinal hope of continual vitality. Peter wrote to the communities in dispersion: "Since you have purified your souls by obeying the truth, in sincere love *(philia)* for the brotherhood you must love *(agape)* one another heartily and fervently, because you have been born anew, not from a *germ* that perishes but from one *that does not perish,* by the word of the living and everlasting God." [7]

---

[7] First Peter 1:22, 23 (C. B. Wms.) Parentheses and italics are mine.

Chapter 6

A Preserving Factor

> Shocking as it is to say so,
> it is important to remember
> that churches can die.
> — *Elton Trueblood*

There have been a few occasions in my life when I have asked myself what it is that keeps a community from falling apart; what essentially preserves its life. The quest is an honest one mainly because I have been the leader of some communities that have fallen apart.

Toward one extreme, we learned — at least in one group — that Christian communities cannot he held together by the mere fact of being together, by being near-kinsmen due to closeness over the years, or by the amenites of social picnics, all of which are relatively uncoercive. At the other extreme, we learned that neither can communities be held together by an imposed, or enforced discipline. More importantly, we discovered the essential factors that break down communication and destroy *koinonia*.

We struggled through, or argued out, in creative conflict together, every crucial problem that arose. Such encounter is not to be discredited. Every community must be capable of dialogue in depth — but when self-life overtakes love, the dialogical dike is left unmanned and the life of the Spirit erodes. Somehow this happened to us, later causing us to wonder (as one person put it) "whether or not Jesus Christ could effect a permanent change in one's life." We are satisfied that Jesus Christ is presently working a permanent change in our lives and that apart from pilgrimage with Him there is no change and no permanency.

In retrospect, a vast array of human elements entered our pilgrimage together. We were all struggling with our own inner battles — personal and spiritual frustrations, family heartaches, vocational pursuits, dreams that challenged us but failed fully to capture us. In trying to bring spiritual health into our own lives we became basically self-oriented again and lost sight of our mission. Sometimes, like damaged cogs in a machine, the raw edges of our humanity met and geared us down.

Here we were — a group of persons who had been related for years in the great Christian perspective. We had known the excitement of daily adventure with Christ. We had ministered to one another and to others over the United States. We had longed to see the day when "church renewal" would be an accomplished fact. Now we were facing the threat of bankruptcy ourselves. The picnics were no longer meeting our casual needs of life together. Our worship became periods of tension; we wanted to be together, but we were afraid that we would do or say something in an inadequate, imperfect way. The periods of confrontation and enforcement toward an inner discipline within community brought our deepest problems to the surface. Once on the surface, rather than loving and forgiving, we somehow unconsciously came to play "God" with one another's needs. We began to dictate to one another. Enforcement caused a reaction to set in to such an extent that when we saw one another we immediately raised the flag of defense. This was not like us. We knew that something was desperately wrong.

It was only after the community decided gradually to cease meeting together, and we were on the outside looking in, that we realized what had happened. We had fallen into a state of ego-inflation that resulted in making us commodities or bargains. We had selfishly tried to pawn our attitudes on one another — and no one wanted to buy.

Retreat became a way of escape. Our picnics largely became flights from our periods of confrontation, over which we had become sick. We were tired of arguing and facing one another down. Escaping into the picnic was easier than breaking through the pride. Even our worship together became one form of retreat from one another — a legitimate, ready-made facade for hiding. Sick unto death, we continued through the motions.

Through this stalemate, we learned that ego-centricity has a way of embellishing itself, of concealing its real feelings in subtle ways. That we could actually cloak these moods in religious sentiment was the chief symptom of our bankruptcy. To both our advantage and disadvantage, we learned that a *projected self-life* is truly a potter's field where love dies; so when the last semblance of life eked out, we "buried" ourselves.

Yet at that point we began to come to life. We had cut the choke-hold that had constricted us. We began to breathe again. Fresh blood began to surge back into our spiritual vessels. Soon, in our better moments alone with God, we knew that we needed one another — desperately needed one another! We saw that we needed the reality and uniqueness and glory that lurked in the shadows of each of us. It was the same reality and uniqueness and glory that we had somehow missed before, because we had looked at one another through carbon-paper eyes. Before, in our *assumed freedom*, we saw one another as "revised editions," "carbon copies," trying to place one another into prefabricated molds. Now, grateful to the God who sets men *free on the inside*, we were looking at one another through the eyes of love and forgiveness.

If a community ever learns the causes and lessons of its defeats, it is well on its way to success. Under Jesus Christ, defeat is always a gateway, never a state of oblivion. "The purpose of acknowledging defeat is not an end in itself but the prelude to having oneself put back together in a new wholeness. In fact the acknowledgment of one's spiritual bankruptcy becomes the open door to growth and spiritual maturity which otherwise could not be achieved."[1]

Since our period of experimentation, each participant has taken up new residence, a new vocational turn, a new spirit of individual pilgrimage, and, surprisingly enough, a new solidarity with one another. In this instance, *koinonia* can be seen existing apart from local association. Perhaps the Spirit of God has chosen to preserve our vitality and relationship by dispersing us to different places in life. Maybe now we must learn how to *minister in dispersion,* not unlike the first adherents of Jesus Christ, who were "the exiles of the Dispersion in Pontus, Galatia, Cappadocia, Asia, and Bithynia, chosen and destined by God the Father and sanctified by the Spirit for *obedience to Jesus Christ* and for sprinkling with his blood." [2] We dared not spoil our lives — for Christ's sake as well as our own.

The impressive observation about the early Christian community is not that it was *born,* but that it became so deeply united as to *preserve* its life and vitality. This is not to imply that it was a perfect, virtuous organism of untried innocence. One needs only to read the accounts in the New Testament regarding the church at Corinth to be assured of this fact. The Christian community learned early in its life, that although it was the "body of Christ," pursuing His life in harmony with and animated by His ethic, there was still the slight possibility that it would always be a *struggling* body. And it always has been. Sometimes, certain expressions of it never make it at all. "Shocking as it is to say so, it is important to remember," writes Trueblood, "that churches can die." [3]

[1] Nat Tracy, Unpublished Summary of "Conference on Spiritual Renewal" (May 2, 3, 1969), No. 28, p. 4. For information on this conference, address all correspondence to Dr. Nat Tracy, Howard Payne College, Brownwood, Texas 76801.

[2] 1 Peter 1:1, 2 (r.s.v.). Italics are mine.

[3] Elton Trueblood, *The Incendiary Fellowship* (New York: Harper & Row, 1967), p. 87.

The same souvenir of thought permeates Christ's message in the book of *Revelation* to the "Seven Churches of Asia Minor." [4] The church at Ephesus, for one, was called upon to remember the heights from which it had "fallen," in that it had lost its ability to love Jesus Christ deeply as at first. Even the church at Smyrna, that still had a rich spirit, was harrassed by "pressing trouble and poverty." In the church at Pergamum, some were being swayed by the teachings of Balaam and the Nicolaitans. There were, also, those in the church at Thyatira, who rather than helping to heal, were tolerating a woman of immorality. Of the church at Sardis it was said: "You have the reputation of being alive, but in reality you are dead." The church at Philadelphia was praised for obeying the true message, yet it was reminded, surreptitiously, of its "little strength." Finally, the church at Laodicea had the disease that will kill any Christian community — it harbored the deadly projection of self-life, the failure to recognize its spiritual bankruptcy. The boast of this church was, "I am rich, I have already become rich, I need nothing."

All of us, no doubt, have met ourselves returning from the church of "Laodicea." The failure to recognize our spiritual bankruptcy before God and men has been the death of us, all too often. Still, the most declarative truth in the universe is that we are, undeniably, *spiritually bankrupt beings.* The problem of "Sin" has dealt us the fatal blow and knuckled us under its power. Spiritual impoverishment is the result of that blow and that power. This is why Nat Tracy has defined "spiritual bankruptcy" as "the incapability of being the master of one's own inner powers because another power has control." [5] "How often we commit certain acts in perfect consciousness," say Paul Tillich, "yet with

[4] Revelation 2–3 (C. B. Wms.).

[5] Nat Tracy, "Conference on Spiritual Renewal" (May 2, 3, 1969), No. 28, p. 3.

the shocking sense that we are being controlled by an alien power!" [6]

Contrary to what we may have thought, our recognition of "Sin" for what it is, is "good news." If "Sin" has left us spiritually bankrupt, it is to our benevolence to know what "Sin" is and how it has defeated us. I am indebted to my teacher, Dr. Tracy, for the explosive insights on "Sin" and my own nature that he has given me.

In the Western world we have a tendency to think in terms of symptoms rather than causes. As a result, "Sin" has been diluted, distorted, and cheapened to mean the whole bastion of iniquities — lying, murder and adultery, to name a few. These are serious, of course, and are not to be regarded lightly, but they are symptoms of a more menacing force in man. Rid ourselves of these and a thousand others take their places because we have not dealt with the insidious *root*. This approach is like chopping limbs off the tree, disregarding the source of its life in the roots. We have simply treated the symptoms and not the disease. Even "rebellion against God" is not definitive for this force, because that too is a by-product or symptom of a more deeply imbedded "disease" of the heart. "Sins" emerge as symptoms of man's inner illness. There is a legitimate distinction.

Ultimately, then, "Sin" is a *mystery*. We do not know where or how it began; we only know that in Lucifer it changed an angelic being into a satanic being, and that it entered the human race through Adam. Yet, we are not so naive as to assume that "Sin" is altogether a hand-me-down from Adam. It does its work all over again in every man, for every man has the same disease of the heart that Adam had. We therefore do not know the mystery of its primal roots, but we know its damage in our lives. Only thus can we come close to an adequate description of it.

Describing it organically, "Sin" is the root-evil or spiritual disease that *causes* dereliction at the center of life. Attitu-

[6] Paul Tillich, *The Shaking of the Foundations* (New York: Charles Scribner's Sons, 1948), p. 159.

dinally, "Sin" may be described as the *cause* of a militant posture of the heart against God. How then does it conduct life toward spiritual bankruptcy? How does it leave me personally defeated?

When I come to the age of self-directedness, or — as many evangelicals have called it — the age of accountability, I invariably become a rebel against God, consciously or unconsciously. If this were not true, there would occasionally appear men who do not bear the symptoms of "Sin." Yet, sinfulness in the human race, as universal, is the most self-validating fact of history; it needs no proof. Moreover, it is *cosmic* in scope, for it does its damage on two frontiers.

The first frontier of "Sin" lies in its attempt to damage that which is contrary to its nature — *God!* To do this, it causes me to shift the center of my dignity from being in God to being in myself. Thus begins a drive to demolish the "image of God" in me, the rightful hub of human existence and human dignity. Under this impact, I set myself up as the guardian of my own life, in which I rise up with foolhardy blindness to affirm, "I will have no God!" or literally, in keeping with the Hebrew text of the Psalmist, "There is not to me a God!" [7]

From this point, I am committed to a moral dilemma — I must act like a "God," for I have taken the destiny of my life into my own hands, but I discover myself incapable of such a role. The way I act and other world conditions are evidence enough.

Not to be outlauded I hold onto my dilemma, which only leads me into the moral predicament of self-delusion. I begin to play-act my self-sufficiency as "God," lying to myself to keep my sanity. My deception, in turn, becomes the gateway to a total stance in hypocrisy of every form.

Then this "kingdom of self" duped by "Sin," obligated to maintain its own sense of worth, sets up a reign in terror, wilfully executing anything or anyone that attempts to gain

[7] Psalm 14:1; 53:1.

the ascendancy over it. I come, finally, to execute God in my heart. The most renegade example of this truth is the crucifixion of Jesus of Nazareth. When He came claiming to be "Lord," men rose up in defiance by putting Him on a cross. This act was a final mutilation of the heart of God, for Jesus Christ is the God-man. It is to this abyss that every man comes, if he does not repent of his rebellious, sanctimonious posture.

The next frontier of "Sin," as if the first were not enough, is the continued attack leveled at God by distorting completely that which is closest to the heart of God — *man!* This becomes more biting still because I become the victim. All the God-inspired properties abundant in my life, which were created within and meant to be turned outward to augment life, are now turned inward to self, and my life begins to languish. I become a contradictory being. Meant to bear an intelligent, moral conscience, I stumble blindly without moral direction. Meant to be a willing, desirous being, I am driven into wrong choices and decisions. Meant to be imaginative and creative, I become uninventive and destructive. Meant to have a clear way toward personal introspection, I deceive myself and gloss over my true state of affairs. Meant to be basically other-centered, I become totally self-centered. Meant to bear rational and moral affection for the giving and receiving of love, I become indifferent or hostile. Meant to be a whole person, I become inwardly divided, in which the false self, created by "Sin," engages the true self, created by God, in a civil war. Meant to be a related being, I become utterly alone; and there is no aloneness like the estrangement I have created without reason.

Against the threat of the cold, dark universe, I become the man who is, as Bonhoeffer has stated, "his own creator, his own judge and his own restorer, the man whose life misses the mark of his own human existence, and who, therefore, sooner or later destroys himself." [8] Having mutilated

[8] Dietrich Bonhoeffer, *Ethics,* ed. by Eberhard Bethge (New York: The Macmillan Company, 1964), p. 46.

the heart of God, I damage my own. Tearfully, I learn that it doesn't pay to be my own God.

Once I recognize my moral abyss as spiritual bankruptcy, I can begin to look for a Savior. Only a Savior can permit me to proceed out of my predicament, otherwise, I end still in self-absorption and egotism.

We can see then what this ego-inflation does to Christian *koinonia.* Rollo May said it well: "If we had no way of overcoming this deep ego-bias, we should be cursed with the necessity of each one's living in the prison of his own private world." [9]

If the regimenting of self-life destroys *koinonia,* then only the recognition of spiritual bankruptcy will spearhead the war in its visible symptoms. Only then, too, can its disaster be nipped in the bud.

One's failure to accept his own impoverishment is the tap-root of such devastating symptoms as *spiritual pride, self-sufficiency,* and *unbridled judgment,* all of which work against community. Until these symptoms have been largely eliminated by cutting the tap-root — through what the living God does for us and continues to do for us — then, community goes the way of downgrade.

We must identify with one another as brothers duped by "Sin," harrassed by its product of self-life, spoiled by its accomplishment of isolation, and know, but for the grace of God, it will make us destroy one another. Our only safeguard is to acknowledge before God and man that we are spiritually impoverished beings.

We must not accept bankruptcy as some attitude of self-defeat, self-nihilism, or sign of unworthiness, but as an avenue of redeeming our humanity rather than destroying it. Not to accept it means a surrender to one's already defeated nature. Thus surrendered, it means the creation and intensification of the aforesaid disabling symptoms that, left to themselves, will destroy the Christian community.

[9] Rollo May, *The Springs of Creative Living* (New York: Abingdon-Cokesbury Press, 1940), p. 217.

Take, for instance, the symptom of *spiritual pride.* The most damaging aspect of spiritual pride is not simply that I think highly of myself, or masquerade in the aura of a self-opinionated goodness. Pride, in its most damaging aspect, is when I have the inner attitude that I can "go it alone" and thereby cut myself off from community. Not only am I no longer open to be taught, but I am no longer free to receive, and, as a consequence, I am no longer subject to giving. I cease being a person with cosmic possibilities; for how can I love and respond to God in whom rests my possibilities, if I cannot love and respond to my brothers in whom those possibilities also reside? It is pretentious to assume that I belong to God, whom I have not seen, if I do not belong to my brothers, whom I have seen. The greatest truth I have ever learned is that I need my brothers, for I am a dependent being.

Spiritual pride thus leads to *self-sufficiency.* When I fail to recognize my need of others, at that point I begin to rise above them superficially. Under the pall of self-sufficiency, destruction of community is imminent, for there can be no *community on a pedestal.*

Out of self-sufficiency comes the other symptom of *unbridled judgment.* Resting on a pedestal, I become defensive of my position and highly critical of those beneath me. Until I recognize that I am neither "inferior," nor "superior" to those next to me, but "equal" to them by virtue of our mutual bankruptcy, immediate reactions of judgment will tend to dominate my life. If I feel inferior, I may destroy community by casually resigning from relationships. Or, on the other hand, because I do feel inferior but must cloak myself, I have the tendency to project myself as superior. Although there is no such thing as "superiority," only a sense of inferiority asserting itself over others, I become judgmental and harsh. Because in reality there is no such thing as "inferiority" either, only *feelings* of inferiority, I make up for my inner feelings of weakness by displaying strong reactions, falsely. In my unbridled judgment, I am unable to give my life to others. I have no deep response to them in relationship, which eventually cuts me off from community.

Paul Tournier, in his book, *Guilt and Grace,* shares a personal observation that is exquisite at this point. He writes:

> How many times I have thought about it when a man has been sobbing in my consulting-room as he has given expression to his disappointment with himself, his faults and failures, his despair and his feelings of inferiority! He is nearer to the Kingdom of God than I who listen to him; and I come nearer — to the Kingdom, as well as to the man — only in so far as I recognize that I am as guilty, as powerless, as inferior and as desperate as he is. Only then also can I help him, for I am delivered from all spirit of judgment, I am his companion in repentance and in waiting for grace. [10]

The spiritual fellowship, unlike all other communities, should transform, intensify, and preserve its own life under Christ. However, such is not always the case, for the suicide of self-life is not that easily carried out. We would like to be Assisis overnight, or instant saints that, like toad-stools, blossom full-grown while men sleep — but irrevocably the turn of our hearts to God is admittedly much slower. Our complete watershed toward God is halting and progressive, to say the least, however cataclysmic our conversion experience or faithful our attendance in a local church. Still, we have banked a great deal on church membership and Christian finery to make us ninety-day wonders for God — never hoping to deal with our basic sinful condition that prevents our becoming so.

Because we delude ourselves so easily, it is difficult to teach one another of our limitations. How do I gain a knowledge of my bankruptcy? I know it when I stand next to God. I am not so sure of it when I stand next to man. The Spirit of God will have to convince me of my bankruptcy,

[10] Paul Tournier, *Guilt and Grace,* trans. by Arthur W. Heathcote, assisted by J. J. Henry and P. J. Allcock (New York: Harper & Brothers, 1962), p. 112.

because it is too subtle on man's part to evict me of my pride. Man can point me to the problem, but as self-centered as I am, he cannot convince me. Nor can he heal me.

The delicate, surgical hand of the Spirit must patiently salvage and heal me in my awareness of bankruptcy. Left to myself, I end in despair; joined to Jesus Christ through the Spirit, there is hope. When through the forgiveness and support of a loving God, I accept His solution to my moral predicament, I am free to venture forth on a deep and realistic level. Little by little, I can unmask in reality to my peers in community, thereby checking the old forms of self-centered power and aggression that creep into its life to destroy it.

If one thing more than anything else augments the preservation of community, it is this recognition of spiritual bankruptcy and the consequent sense of reality provided by it. In the last analysis, it is not an absence of problems, but the acceptance of dying as a part of living that gives to community its memoirs.

Chapter 7

The Healing Force

> It is recognized that what is past cannot be restored by any human might, and that the wheel of history cannot be turned back. Not all the wounds inflicted can be healed, but what matters is that there shall be no further wounds.
>
> — *Dietrich Bonhoeffer*

If the New Testament is clear on anything, it is clear on the essential meaning of forgiveness and its indispensability for social, moral and spiritual health. Contrary to what many believe, its basic purpose is not to *pardon* but to *heal*. At least in the New Testament its aim is always that of redemption and healing. Even the purpose for which Christ Himself became the embodiment of forgiveness was that men might be *made whole*.

In the *Eye Opener,* a magazine of the McAlester, Oklahoma Prison System, one column had the solicitous caption: "Pardon Me." While this may be humorous in the light of prison life, the implications are quite realistic. In a tour of another state correctional institution, I noticed in conversation with several prisoners that each talked of being pardoned and released, while none talked of being healed.

Many who were in for the second and third offenses were demonstrations in point that what men need is a radical transformation, not just a periodic transfusion. Men need correction, not control. Later, in a personal letter to one of the prisoners with whom I had formed a basic friendship, I wrote in part: "I am hoping that you are learning more and more every day what it means to be part of society and are coming to grips with the role you must assume when you are released. I am praying that the *real* you, the *constructive* you, will be brought to light by your stay in the Department of Corrections."

That men need more than amnesty or indulgence is manifestly the reason for which Christ came. He offered men a healing force. His final hope for men was not that they be *acquitted,* so much as that they be *atoned.* Whereas acquittal is a one-time transaction, atonement begins a process of "restoring to wholeness." It is a process of healing inaugurated from the core outward. "God's pardon is not a static attribute," says Tournier, "but a movement, a drive." [1]

Any Christian community that will be a healing force in society, must possess and demonstrate Christ's spirit of forgiveness. As the community receives His kind of forgiveness, it becomes healed, and as it gives His kind of forgiveness, it becomes healing. What is elemental, therefore, is a long hard look at the manner in which Christ forgave men. It will bring us to some corrective measures of our own.

An initial and major corrective is that which deals with man's guilt and God's justice. Men needed a decisive recognition of their guilt. Christ, therefore, did not condone the offenses of men. In order to be a healing force in their lives, He awakened them unapologetically to the reality of their guilt.

A large segment of society holds the misconception that Christ offered men forgiveness out of a large-hearted weakness. They suggest that He waived men's offenses by a moral

[1] Paul Tournier, *Guilt and Grace*, p. 145.

juggling of justice, by an almost condoning spirit, by merely letting them off the hook. Nothing could be farther from the truth. In Jesus Christ, there is no condoning spirit and, balanced with that, no condemning attitude. Yet justice always holds sway in His forgiving acts. At any rate, men found healing in His presence, but never any aspect that produced feelings of false guilt or unworthiness. By His forgiveness Christ unleashed men spiritually to walk erect into the sunlight of freedom, but He always left the moral principle, "Sin no more!" ringing in their ears. Whereas a condoning spirit would not have required such a principle, a spirit of justice must consider the guilt of man if he is to be helped.

The New Testament will neither allow us to skip over the need for justice, nor to evade Christ's principle of integrity. Consider the man whom Christ healed at the Pool of Siloam when He met the religious authorities and refused to bear the responsibility for having been healed on the Sabbath — incidentally laying the blame on Christ. Christ sought him out and forgave him with the words: "Behold, thou art made whole: sin no more, lest a worse thing come unto thee." [2] Christ did not send this man on his way without first arousing concern over his lack of integrity. Although he could accept the *man*, he could not condone his *irresponsibility*. While there was affirmation of the person, there was also repudiation of the sin.

The same is virtually true of the Samaritan woman at Jacob's well. Christ accepted her, not only apart from the religious scruples mounting between Jew and Samaritan, but also in spite of her life of prostitution in the city of Sychar. He kindly led her to the moral issue: "Go get thy husband!" Of course, she had no husband, and Christ easily sensed it. But His attitude was of such captivating warmth that she felt free to talk to Him. During the dialogue, the woman came to grips with her guilt. She sensed His forgive-

[2] John 5:14 (K.J.V.).

ness and accepted it with integrity of action. Forgetting her water jar at the well, she hurried back into the city announcing Christ to the men there as "one who has told me everything that ever I did." [3]

On another occasion, the scribes and Pharisees brought to Christ a woman whom they had taken in the very act of adultery. They intended that He stone her according to the ancient law of Moses. He, in fact, forgave her! Let her accusers stone her! But they could not, for they, as much as she, were awakened to the reality of their own guiltiness. The awkward silence of Christ thundered home to their misguided hearts. The greater injustice would be for Christ to have judged the one whose accusers bore the greater sin — *the inability to love unconditionally.* Because Christ knew that condemnation is anything but healing, He could abandon this woman to her own judgment with the words: "Neither do I condemn thee: go, and sin no more." [4]

There is little therapy in justice alone. Healing comes when love is added. Paul Tillich had part of the truth when he said that "man can believe in forgiveness only if justice is maintained and guilt is confirmed." [5] But the other half of the truth is that men can believe in forgiveness only when love and justice form a cognate. As we pointed out in a previous chapter, real love is strong love, and real strength is merciful. Love without righteousness is indulgent. Righteousness without love is merciless. Righteous-love is an important combination, for it is *the way grace acts* — justly and lovingly. Was C. H. Spurgeon aware of this when he preached: "Justice awards me nothing but death; grace alone can bring me life"? [6]

For Christ to forgive a world pulled apart by strife, certainly could not mean by any stretch of the imagination that

[3] John 4:1-42.
[4] John 8:11 (K.J.V.).
[5] Paul Tillich, *Systematic Theology* (Chicago: The University of Chicago Press, 1951), I, p. 288.
[6] C. H. Spurgeon, *The Metropolitan Tabernacle Pulpit* (London: Passmore & Alabaster, 1908), XV, p. 195.

He was a party to disharmony in the world community, or that He was embellishing inner division. He did not varnish over moral violations for the sake of a more reputable appearance. He forgave such moral disorder because it was the only roadmap to sanity and wholeness. He found it quite useless to fight fire with fire. Instead He swept men off balance by igniting their emotions with mercy. With a remarkable touch, He brought quiet into men's lives. He chose the artillery of *a new violence* — the violence of love.

Men could not understand the *fight of friendship*, especially when there was no apparent reason why one should expend himself for the sake of others. And yet, the very characteristic approach of Christ was that of a conciliating advance which disarmed antagonism. Here, indeed, was a man for the health of other men.

A second corrective essential to the meaning of forgiveness (briefly mentioned in chapter 2) is that it is unconditional in nature. Jesus did not set forth certain conditions for men before He would forgive them. Forgiveness was present before they asked. God, having *already* reconciled Himself to the world, was (and is) now in Christ "reconciling the world unto himself." [7] The only condition necessary was men's *acceptance* of His forgiveness for making it operative in their lives. This alone kept it from universal indulgence.

The most unlikely specimens of humanity, men and women who were in desperate need of forgiveness, Jesus invited into healing partnership with Himself. "Come, follow me," was His open invitation. The surprising note was that He never retracted His forgiveness *when men refused to follow.* He *never took Himself back* because men did not choose Him. Somehow He left the impression that men, to be cherished as persons, need not meet His demands. The greatest possible sign of acceptance and the wisest possible way for healing to take place in men's lives was for Christ

[7] 2 Corinthians 5:19.

to present Himself in such unconditional light that men drew near enough to enter into a redemptive, healing relationship. More than all else His forgiveness brought soundness and integration into shattered lives.

As a student in college I learned from a group of friends just how healing unconditional forgiveness can be. I had a chance to preach to the Saturday night "Youth for Christ" fellowship in our church. For a week I prepared, polished and trimmed, memorized and all but mimed my sermon. Then I got up to preach. Painfully I lobbed my verbal foliage over the pulpit to about the first pew. Not a leaf of it fell on a soul but instead it settled lifelessly to the floor. I made mistakes of every imaginable kind. My communication was rigid, canned, affectatious. I failed miserably. When I had finished I rushed out of the auditorium into the choir room behind and wept. Many of my friends followed and tried to console me. I confessed failure — and the greatest thing they ever did for me was not to pull me into self-pity by saying, "Oh, that was a fine message." It would have been a lie and I was already pitying myself too much. Instead, they said, "It doesn't matter" — and that healed me.

Read the compelling story in Genesis of how Joseph was sold into Egyptian slavery by his older brothers. Later when he was advanced as the right-hand man of the Pharaoh of Egypt he said to his famished brothers: "Do not be distressed, or angry with yourselves, because you sold me here." [8] There is free love and forgiveness.

It is this free love and forgiveness, says Paul Tournier, "which bowls us over, frees us from the burden of guilt, transforms us, provokes 'metanoia' [repentance]." [9] Whenever this fact has been discovered in history, Tournier reminds us, there has been an outburst of spiritual renewal. The renewal has come because unconditional forgiveness has brought healing with it. Relationships are re-established at the core, a new mind and spirit are generated, the weight

[8] Genesis 45:5 (R.S.V.).
[9] Paul Tournier, *Guilt and Grace*, p. 193. Brackets are explanatory.

of spiritual illness is lifted. Men are actually touched deeply enough as to become healing forces in return.

Strangely, when we, through the anomaly of unconditional forgiveness, "change our minds" (metanoia) about *God,* about *ourselves,* and about the *world,* it does something of lasting significance within us and life begins to take on overtones of abundance.

This happened in the experience of a gentleman who related to me the following story. He told me of his sister who had been coaxed into sexual involvement by one of her teachers, a married man. The relationship ended with her taking the brunt of the scandal. Understandably, when her brother learned of it, the shock left him raging. Things settled for awhile after the initial blow and following the measures taken by the school board — but the gnawing inside didn't die. Bitterness and resentment took hold to such extent that one day as he drove through the city where the teacher lived, his hostility almost got the best of him. He even had thoughts of taking violent measures to avenge the hurt of his family. "For a long time afterward," he said, "I hated this man — until I realized that if I wanted to keep my sanity, I would have to forgive him." As he was telling me his story I could see signs of the past hurt, but I could also see signs of a man being freed to love. I realized then that only God can cause us to change our minds so healing can begin to take place.

The meaning of the "unconditionalism" of God toward His creatures is best illustrated by an experiment undertaken by a lady in one of our groups. She shared openly one of her most intensely personal struggles. Flanked with the endless menial chores of child-rearing and housekeeping, she felt that she had had it with God. Touched deeply by her doubt of God's love, with intermittent tears that actually sparkled in her beauty, Lori told the group:

"I detest the fact that God allowed me to have *twins.* The care of crying babies, of an older child, of cooking, of ironing, of keeping a husband going, and all the rest — no woman should be subjected to such torture. Sometimes I hate God (I'm telling you how I feel now); sometimes I feel like going into the yard and shaking my fist in God's face and saying, 'I hate You, God.' "

No amount of explanation on the part of the group regarding the natural laws of childbirth could salve her feelings of hostility toward God. She was looking for support on a level deeper than the intellectual. While attempting to show acceptance and concern for the deep throbbing in her life, I recalled what Francois Fénelon once wrote: "If God bores you, tell Him so." Almost spontaneously I broke into the silence that by this time had overcast the group.

"Lori," I spoke up, "you and I know that God knows your feelings already. Perhaps, then, the best thing you could do when you have these feelings which you have just described, is to do as you feel — go out into your yard, shake your fist in God's face and tell Him you hate Him, and see if it *makes any difference* to God in His acceptance and love for you."

During the next group session there came a very rewarding and quite unexpected announcement. Emotions ran high as Lori shared with the group how she had actually tried the suggestion by venting her hostilities to God in her back yard.

"All the scorn in me came out," she said, "and I told God I hated Him, giving every reason why I should. And with me" (there was a pause, a silence, the wiping of tears, and then she continued) ". . . with me — well, it punctured my self-centered balloon and broke my heart; but with God, I discovered, it made no difference! He still loves me . . . and I believe I love Him, too!"

In his book, *The Art of Understanding Yourself,* Cecil Osborne relates a number of personal experiences of people who have found healing and new hope in some of the spiritual growth groups. The result of one such experience came to him expressed in a letter by a nurse in an Eastern city. This person related that the greatest thing which had come to her from the group was the lesson of love learned through the expression of those who loved and cared unconditionally. She went on to underscore something of extreme importance in the art of love:

> I had been so hurt by parents who cut me to ribbons that I never learned to give or receive love. They said they would love me if I got the best marks in school. They would slap me and then say, "But we love you." Love based on an "if" or a "but" is never love. [10]

Dr. Osborne reminds us in his book, that "it is love which heals, for love is of God, and it is through love that He performs His miracles of healing." [11]

To have this quality of love in the Christian community is an all-important healing catalyst. Every Christian acting as one grain of salt can do a lot of healing. "When this *one* person practices forgiveness in a company that is poisoned by intrigue and enmity," says Helmut Thielicke, "then all of a sudden there is a healing factor in the situation." [12]

In his second letter to the Christian community at Corinth, [13] Paul affirms that the act of forgiveness is that attitude of response which "makes love valid." Returning to forgive is that quality in a person, which, according to another translation "confirms love *(agape).*" Of all the New Testament writers, Paul alone uses this word *(kerosai).* It expressly carries implications of "unconditionalism." The remaining use of the word is its passive form in Galatians 3:15, used to describe a contract of agreement that has been

[10] Cecil G. Osborne, *The Art of Understanding Yourself* (Grand Rapids, Mich.: Zondervan Publishing House, 1967), p. 187.

[11] *Ibid.,* p. 187.

[12] Helmut Thielicke, *Life Can Begin Again: Sermons on the Sermon on the Mount,* trans. by John W. Doberstein (Philadelphia: Fortress Press, 1963), p. 30.

[13] 2 Corinthians 2:6-8.

ratified or *confirmed,* whereupon there can be no annulment or change. Forgiveness, as the "confirming of love," is therefore an unconditional act, foundational to bringing healing and harmony into fractured relationships, much the same as a ratified contract is meant to resolve any unforeseen complications among legal transactions. Paul was calling upon the Christian community to reaffirm its love to one who had been censored from the community. His call shows that the absence of forgiveness means also the absence of love. "Only love is strong enough to forgive," writes Dr. William Parker, "and if we deny our own forgiveness to anyone, are we not denying Love's presence within us? Where then is our *healing power?*" [14]

Unconditionalism seeks a remedy, not a penalization. The "father" in the story of the "Prodigal Son" is no penal authority or potentate who demands reparations from his wayward son. His love is *remedial* instead of *jurisprudent.* He gives his son what he *needs* instead of what he *deserves.* Such amiable response serves as the healing force for the emptiness of heart. The ensuing atmosphere of this story could never have been a mark of acquittal or cheap surrender; it could only have been the mark of an unconditional spirit blossoming entirely new. There is nothing *chiropractic* about forgiveness; it does not try to heal by manipulation. It rather leaves one free to decide how he will answer the question: "Wilt thou be made whole?" The son had been left free to decide.

The prodigal is asked back into relationship as a *son,* to him an unexpected turn, for he would have gladly welcomed the menial status of a *servant.* He is received into home and hearth, when all he might have expected was a bunk in the hireling quarters. A forgiveness that seeks restoration and healing, but never privation, is the white heat that "bowls him over," and (in a borrowed phrase) "melts

---

[14] William R. Parker and Elaine St. Johns, *Prayer Can Change Your Life* (Englewood Cliffs, N. J.: Prentice-Hall, Inc., 1957), p. 217. Italics are mine.

his heart." No one can withstand that kind of intensity. Nothing is more healing and demanding than the forgiving act of one who affirms our being when we are sick of ourselves. Nothing is so jolting to us as when someone "makes merry" over us when we feel like weeping. Such a reversal of the ordinary, expected reaction is understandable only of a "heavenly Father," and sometimes of an earthly one. Yet, insomuch as the Christian community is called upon to witness to this kind of reversal, it may, under Christ, become the healing community.

Third, forgiveness is no spiritual panacea. We would be naive to assume that it remedies all our ills, or even that it intercepts all the consequences of our sinfulness. The manner in which Jesus Christ forgives us, permits us to forgive ourselves, to accept ourselves as we are, and to live in the attitude of this "realized forgiveness." It does not, however, promise to eliminate the consequences of our wrong deeds. The miracle of Christ's forgiveness lies in the fact that it arrests the *causes* of the wounds imposed and their further destructive powers. We certainly need to know that there is a *cure*, a power that does more than alleviate the symptoms of sin and their consequences.

For this reason, I do not totally subscribe to remarks by one writer who, in his best-selling book, observes that forgiveness cuts away the wrong as if it had never been done. The same must follow with another writer who suggests that forgiveness restores broken relationships as though they had never been broken. What is viable and essential is that men accept the wrong done as an *actual event* in their lives, not as though it had never been done, but *as an event made anemic and powerless in their lives* by the acceptance of forgiveness. This kind of forgiveness does not *wash out* the event by cheap grace, but risks a kind of ruthless surgery, kindly administered, which sutures and dresses the wound while it weeps over the loss. Perhaps this is what Dietrich Bonhoeffer meant when he wrote: "It is recognized that what is past cannot be restored by any human might, and that the wheel of history cannot be turned back. Not all the wounds inflicted can be healed, but what matters is that there shall be no further wounds." [15]

What is needed then is a cure and not a pampered peace — a strengthening and not a state of amnesty. The Christian community may become a healing force in society if it can obtain and deploy the strengthening quality of Christ's forgiveness. The strength of Christ's forgiveness is that He does not simply hand out *pardons* for my sinful acts, leaving me maimed morally and spiritually. His forgiveness is rather a costly enterprise in that He forgives me for *being* the kind of person who can harbor sinful acts and then *involves* himself with me until a new "law" begins to dominate my life — the law of love and forgiveness. For Christ to undertake such an unlikely venture, means the willful tying of Himself to me so that He reconstructs on the human level the "life" of God within me.

Without Christ's intercession, I falter blindly, remain unhealed, and increasingly live after the laws of remorse and revenge. Remorse allows me to *repeat my sins* in abject slavery, and excuses me for being *human.* Revenge allows me to think that I am still *master,* and makes up the difference for not being *God.* The truth is, though, I am neither human enough to handle my own life, nor divine enough to handle God's. Therefore, I need Jesus Christ far more than He needs me. That I survive my sins because *I believe in Jesus Christ,* may be altogether true, but it is equally true that I survive them because *Jesus Christ believes in me.* He keeps on forgiving me, and believing in me until one day He transforms me. This is the strength of Christ: "that He who began the good work in (me) will go on until the day of Jesus Christ to complete it." [16]

It is not simply humorous then to say that God is calling the Christian community into the *survival business*—through

[15] Dietrich Bonhoeffer, *Ethics*, pp. 53-54.
[16] Philippians 1:6 (C. B. Wms.).

it believing in and reaching out to broken humanity, expecting the best of recovery for every bleeding heart, and offering forgiveness as the healing balm.

The art of healing, far more than we know, lies in the dictum of Paul: "Be kind to one another, tenderhearted, forgiving one another, as God in Christ forgave you." [17]

---

[17] Ephesians 4:32 (R.S.V.).

Chapter 8

Feeling Private

> The church has, to a large
> extent unconsciously, retreat-
> ed within its own borders: *it
> has become itself a world.*
> How to break out again from
> isolation into communication
> with the world is becoming
> an urgent concern for many
> in the churches. [1]
>
> — *Kathleen Bliss*

There was a time when I argued that a man could become
a Christian *apart from the church.* I remember debating
this issue at Laity Lodge with Dr. Myron Madden, chaplain
of one of the large hospitals in New Orleans and author of
The Power to Bless. He took the opposite position and, I
now admit, rightly so. In fact, he told me then, that if I
would give it some serious thought, I would soon come to his
position — and he was not speaking dogmatically.

Part of my problem had been that I was always shooting
for the ideal explanation and nearly always missed the forest
for the trees. "Ideally," I would say, "a man living in the
hills apart from any church, with only a Testament in his
hands, could discover Christ and become a Christian." Actu-

[1] Kathleen Bliss, *We The People* (Philadelphia: Fortress Press, 1964),
p. 17.

ally, that was always a true statement, because I knew that no one had to be a member of a local congregation to find faith in Christ. My theological position, in fact, was that a man did not submit to local church membership until he had attested to a personal experience of faith in Christ.

What I had never considered was how the man in the hills got his Testament to begin with, or even the occasion for the Testament itself. When I faced these issues, I uncovered my fallacy — the New Testament did not create the early church; the early church produced the New Testament. Men in the fellowship of Christ, under the inspiration of the Spirit, gave to us the writing of the New Testament. Indirectly then, a man was dependent on the church.

What I had never considered, also, was the real nature of the church. My fallacy here was the incessant pull to think in terms of a local congregation rather than what it means to "be" the church. When I contemplated the church as the "body of Christ," or as the "fellowship of Christ," I had to back down in my argument once again — the church by definition was *an organism dependent on relationships.* It certainly was never meant to be an institution from which men could easily segment their lives simply by leaving the parking lot. To be a Christian meant to be part of this universal body of believers.

I had to recall, moreover, just how instrumental even the local church had been in my own conversion. My conclusion, now totally in line with Dr. Madden's, was that we never become Christians alone. There are no solitary Christians.

In my theological expertise, I almost overlooked the most conspicuous support of all. Man cannot even be man apart from experience with other men. He unendingly needs a personal, spiritual relationship because he is a personal, spiritual being. He can neither live apart from his fellow creatures nor from his Creator and fulfill that for which he was designed. He is, incurably, an interrelated being. Paul, writing to the Romans, said: "None of us lives to himself, and none of us dies to himself." [2] We are all dependent beings, dependent on everything and on everyone. George Hendry was correct then when he said that "personal being is essentially being in relation, not being in isolation." [3]

Man cannot be an island and remain healthy in any sense. To remain isolated would be to digress more and more toward the primitive. My colleague in the ministry, Creath Davis, has in his book (*Beyond This God Cannot Go*) a chapter entitled, "Isolation Is Insanity." In it he states: "If an infant could be physically cared for without any kind of human relationship, he would be less than human. His personality would never develop, and he would act like an animal. . . . We are always just one generation away from barbarism. Our relationships furnish the necessary orientation to life so that every culture may progress."[4] A prime example of this is the discovery some years ago of two children in the forests of France, who ran with the wolves; indeed, they had been reared by them. Brought into captivity, they displayed every sign of the primitive. They ran on all fours, growled at their captors and howled in the night. Having begun without any kind of human relationship, these children made no "human" progress. They were living against the grain of man's intended nature.

A more current example centers around a man I knew who for a number of years, conditioned himself to live apart from normal relationships. When I first knew him, he seldom went into town. Later, he stopped altogether and sent his wife instead. She was beginning to have emotional disturbances herself because their relationship had diminished with age. I recall passing their house many times and seeing him seated in his automobile reading a paper or staring into the distance for hours at a time. I would go to his house, knowing that he was home, but he would not answer the door.

2 Romans 14:7 (r.s.v.).

3 George S. Hendry, *The Gospel of the Incarnation* (Philadelphia: The Westminster Press, 1958), p. 105.

4 Creath Davis, *Beyond This God Cannot Go* (Grand Rapids, Mich.: Zondervan Publishing House, 1971), pp. 81-82.

The last time I saw this man, he had lost all ability to relate in an adequate verbal manner. Over a period of three or four years, I stood by helplessly watching his digression to an almost primitive state.

Karl Menninger, the renowned psychiatrist, points up that "the man with no friends has already abandoned himself to the fate of his own self-destructiveness." He goes on to say that "psychiatrists realize from clinical experience . . . that to retreat permanently into the loneliness of one's own soul is to surrender one's claim upon life." [5]

Sociologists have a similar point of view when they differentiate between man's "organic" needs and his "sociogenic" needs. Sociogenic needs are derived from a group-consciousness in man. Ogburn and Nimkoff state: "Prominent among these acquired needs, largely built up around the ego, are the desire to belong to the group, to be accepted and loved by the group, and to enjoy good standing in the group." In addition, they state that "when an individual withdraws from association with other human beings, he is likely to be or to become queer. If his withdrawal from others is extreme, it may mean insanity. Clearly the sociogenic drives are highly important motivating forces in personality." [6]

In the realm of the personal, Christian psychiatrists are advising persons more and more today against a too liberal introspection. Man's maturity and mental health, they claim, depend upon an attitude of "otherness," which frees him from a too radical self-preoccupation. As early as 1940 Rollo May observed that one of the most common ways of liberating man from his egocentricity, is through the possibility open to him of responding to the need of his fellow-men. Enlarging his observation, he wrote: "This grace through our fellow-men is an expression of the logos in us, in that we were created in community. Adam and Eve lived in com-

[5] Karl Menninger, *Love Against Hate* (New York: Harcourt, Brace & World, Inc., 1942), p. 271.

[6] William F. Ogburn & Meyer F. Nimkoff, *Sociology* (Boston, Mass.: Houghton Mifflin Company, 1950), second edition, p. 217.

munity; until the fall they did not feel 'private'; and it is of
the essence of ourselves and an aspect of our ultimate destiny
that we live in community." [7]

Feeling "private" has also become one of the tremendous
hazards facing the church today. Quite possibly, the epi-
graph that heads this chapter is a valid cross-section of everyone's suspicion that the church is a microcosm all its own.
At least intellectual assent to this proposition is almost universal at this point. The contention has been that we have
isolated ourselves in our little Christian societies almost as
if we belonged to a private club. Having the welcome mat
out does not seem to change the situation.

The church has faced this problem throughout its history.
Illustrative of the fact is John Wycliffe, in the fourteenth
century, who called the Medieval monasteries "castles of
Cain," precisely because they were expressions of the
church's retreat from the world and danger. He properly
asserted that Christ never intended for Christians to hide in
cloisters.

The same bias toward solidarity with the world should
appeal to the church today. In many instances, it does not.
A recent survey taken by sociologist Jeffrey K. Hadden,
shows that of six major denominations in America, there is a
positive concensus that the church should exist for man
rather than withdrawing from the world. In the sampling, an
average of seventy-two percent of those answering the survey were in agreement with the statement: *"The Christian
church can only be its true self as it exists for humanity,*
while an average of only eight percent agreed with the
second statement: *"The primary task of the church is to live
the Christian life among its own membership and activities
rather than try and reform the world."* [8] The response here,
however, appears to be one of ideal approval or theoretical

---

[7] Rollo May, *The Springs of Creative Living*, p. 215.

[8] Jeffrey K. Hadden, *The Gathering Storm in the Churches* (Garden City,
N.Y.: Doubleday & Company, Inc., 1969), tables 20-21, pp. 57-58.

belief. Undoubtedly, there is a tremendous discrepancy between what Christians approve of or *believe* about the role
of the church and what they actually *practice.*

If consensus among Christians leans more strongly toward
involvement and communication with the world, then the
question is forthcoming: "Why is involvement and communication with the world not more widespread than it appears to be?" If it is not taken to be too simplistic, the answer is that we have lost the magnificence of what it means
to be a "servant people."

It goes without question that when the church loses the
precise role for which it exists, it becomes merely another
organization. When it loses its rightful expression as a "fellowship of servants," it also loses its life as an *organism.* It
is not difficult to find Christ's "Body" solidifying into church
machinery today. Much of the time, the church is preoccu-
pied with brainstorming for stylish "techniques" of interchange with the world, while its *concern* becomes little more
than the perfunctory work of enterprising committees. If
we have thought that mere organization or programming
communicates devotion, we are in for a sobering surprise.
Candid ministry to the needs of people alone communicates
concern. As Woodrow Wilson put it: "You know that nothing communicates fire except fire."

I was conversing once with Dr. Jack Gray [9] in the cor-
ridors of Scarborough Hall on the Campus of Southwestern
Seminary. I raised the perplexing question of the Christian's
inability to communicate his life today. "Why has the church
largely lost its winsomeness in this vital area?" I asked.
Smiling sympathetically at my ignorance, Dr. Gray gently
grasped the lapels of my coat with both hands, drew me
toward himself and whispered: "We do not *communicate*
because we do not *care!*"

The emphasis placed on those two words did not go without impact, because for the moment I was the "Christian"

---

[9] A very cordial friend, Dr. Gray is professor of Missions at Southwestern Baptist Theological Seminary, Fort Worth, Texas.

squared away in hand. You really must listen when someone talks into your eyes what he reads from your heart. It
took no specialization on the part of Dr. Gray to point up
the patent syndrome of many clergy and laity alike — the
inability to love deeply.

Probably no specialization is needed, likewise, to see that
an "uncaring" church is a "non-communicating" church —
and as a result, an "ingrown," "dying" church. In at least
two fellowships, when we stopped going on mission, reaching
out to others and loving them, we began to atrophy as centers of spiritual life. We learned that apart from a recognition of our own "spiritual bankruptcy," the need to be a
"servant people" outside the community of faith is the sole
nourishment that keeps it alive.

If "servanthood" is an antidote for religious isolationism,
then we need to understand its nature and how we may have
it. There are certain positive and negative aspects that need
to be mentioned.

First, servanthood can marshal its own kind of arrogance,
becoming motivated by total self-gratification. In this case,
it is not the answer to our feeling private but a more insidious expression of it. Servanthood that is not "other-centered"
is not really servanthood at all, for it *alienates* before it has
a chance to *communicate.*

Following a Prayer Therapy group meeting which I was
leading, one of the participants brought this issue home to
me by asking rather pointedly: "Do you think that sometimes we serve people for the sheer sake of our own ego-
inflation?" All of us who would serve know how to be sensitive to such a question. I haltingly answered the person's
question but not without sensitivity: first, because I did not
really have an adequate answer, and second, because there
had been times when I had felt conscious of the joy I was
receiving out of service to others. Since that evening I have
been interested to find others who share in the same feelings.
Paul Tournier, in one of his striking confessions, set my heart
at ease:

A certain more or less conscious egoism always lurks behind the pleasure one derives from devoting oneself to others. I am only too well aware of it in my profession of service to others! It gives me pleasure, a pleasure no different from that sought by people who are accused of being selfish because they are interested only in themselves. My devotion is no more disinterested. [10]

We must never forget the truth that each of us is a potential mutation from *Narcissus*. Everyone recalls Ovid's story of Narcissus and the disenchantment he had with everything except his own beauty. The love of many maidens made him no less self-attentive. The nymph Echo, in love with Narcissus, was so overshadowed and hurt by his indifference that all but her voice faded away. For this, the anger of the gods mounted against him and he was made to fall in love with his own reflection in a pool of water. No matter how he tried, self-admiration prevented his leaving the pool. Subsequently, Narcissus died and became the flower that bears his name.

Seeing our reflection in the "pool of service" may not be grossly damaging; falling in love with it, on the other hand, is fatal to any significant interchange between persons.

The tragedy comes in servanthood, then, when self-indulgence becomes the central motive. On the other hand, the person who knows he has served meaningfully but does not feel some amount of significance and excitement, is as unfortunate as the person who knows he has served profitably but who pretends a disinterested modesty. Conscious awareness of service does not mean impurity of heart and motive any more than disinterested service does.

This leads us to the second aspect — the counterpart of the first one: *Servanthood demands a healthy egoism.* Any avid student of the New Testament knows the premium the Word places on a proper love of oneself. A healthy egoism is indispensable to any proper concern for others. Our nega-

[10] Paul Tournier, *A Place For You*, trans. by Edwin Hudson (New York: Harper & Row, 1966), pp. 108-109.

ting our own self-worth would only damage what otherwise might have been a gift to others. "Love thy neighbor as thyself" is no injunction against one's own value and uniqueness. Rather, it is a solicitation to love *that "self" which one is becoming in the living Christ.* When a person begins to see himself as Christ sees him — without rejection — then he is better able to see others with the same generous eyes. In so doing, he is then free to love others without the traditionally sordid attitude of self-abnegation. The outworn admonition to love God first, others second, and ourselves last, is a false injunction.

We must never forget the age-old truth about man — that he needs both to love and to be loved. The response of others who affirm him is a necessary support. There is, moreover, no incongruity between loving and being loved. Love in fact begets love. It is strange that I should find this confirmed from the writing of an authenticated atheist — Karl Marx, the founder of Communism. Still, he had the nucleus of devotion correct when he wrote: "If you love without calling forth love, that is, if your love as such does not produce love, if by means of an expression of life as a loving person you do not make of yourself a loved person, then your love is impotent, a misfortune." [11] Love is never self-denial!

Third, spontaneity is the logic of servanthood. Technically, the best service we have ever rendered is probably when it has been conveyed somewhat as electricity transmits its energy — silently. That silent power has made "many a dynamo" a *servant* to civilization. Our greatest significance, therefore, may have come when we have been totally unaware of some instinctive assistance, while our greatest failure may have come when we have been certain that we were the people's "finest hour." Perhaps our problem at this point is that we sometimes take servanthood *too* seriously — like kindly escorting the elderly lady across the street only to find that she did not want to cross the street. Service

---

[11] Translation from the German by Eric Fromm, *The Sane Society* (New York: Holt, Rinehart & Winston, Inc., 1955), p. 132.

becomes unnatural when it becomes improvisive rather than instinctive. When it is made an addendum to life rather than an extension of personality etched into the character by Christ, it becomes misconstrued. Many times we utilize the Christian ethic of "doing unto others" out of a Christian determinism merely because it is considered part of the Gospel. We often fail to check whether our heart accepts the cause as something it really desires to do or simply follows as an indifferent tag-along. The result is a service monitored by spiritual immaturity.

When we must command forth our concern, spontaneity gives way to self-consciousness, and the result is an unnatural flow of spiritual adrenalin. On the other hand, when servanthood arises unstructured and uncoerced, it is usually a consequence of the "servant spirit." That spirit is not of our own doing; it must be galvanized into our character by Jesus Christ.

The fourth aspect, then, is that *servanthood is the work of Christ in us*. Who among us feels equal to Christ's unmatched "spirit of servanthood"? Yet Paul wrote in Philippians:

> Keep on bearing this in mind in yourselves, which was also in Christ Jesus, who though being in the form of God did not regard his being on equality with God a thing to be selfishly grasped; but by accepting the form of a *servant* emptied himself, having come to be in the likeness of men; and having been found in fashion as a man he humbled himself by becoming obedient unto death, even the death of a cross. [12]

Fostering this disposition is possible only as we become dependent upon the inner witness of Christ in our lives. Stark humanism is vain because this desire to *empty* oneself for the sake of the world is not human but divine.

The greatest thrill of my Christian venture has been those times when someone has come to me and said: "You may

[12] Philippians 2:5-8 (personal translation).

not realize this, but you served me admirably the other day when you . . . " — and then they would state their case. The enriching thrill has been to assure me that Jesus Christ actually is energizing my character beneath the scene. Even during those times when I have been "out of it" he has championed my spirit and allowed me to "entertain strangers unawares."

If the church can serve as Christ served, it can communicate its life. Perhaps that is the place to begin! There where we discover servanthood at its best! Servanthood, with its ability to communicate, can be no richer than our perception of it in Christ. If in Christ we could but determine the extent to which God has offered Himself to the world as the Servant of all men, we could better understand our own degree of commitment to it. Our commitment will emerge as partial and halting, to say the least; but if moral integrity may be called to bear, a continual response to Christ to be made servants will carry us beyond mediocrity.

God has loved us, has met our needs, and most of us in the church have accepted His mercy with indulgence. To remain deliberately on this plateau is unthinkable. God's interminable grace is focused on making us other-centered beings, for essential to His nature is an intrinsic bias toward servanthood. From this moral center everything in creation takes its meaning — even our privacy.

Chapter 9

The Indispensable Community

> "You are the salt of the
> earth. . . . You are the light
> of the world."
> — Matthew 5:13a, 14a (R.S.V.)

Since the time of Christ, the penetration of society by the church has always been characterized by the symbols "salt" and "light." Many threadbare platitudes have grown up around these two symbols. A few more in this chapter could do no greater harm. Yet there is hope in the observation that Christ never intended His simile of the church as salt and light to be platitudinous. He actually meant for His followers to act as salt and light upon the world. Far from being commonplace He in fact intended that they *be* salt and light to the world.

Dietrich Bonhoeffer distinguished salt as "the most indispensable necessity of life." He went on to characterize the Christian disciples, whom Christ called "the salt of the earth," as "the supreme value which the earth possesses, for without them it cannot live." [1]

On the surface, this is a "hard saying," offensive to the out-and-out cynic and to the non-Christian world. Once I was sharing with a couple in California what Christ and the Christian faith meant to me and what it could mean for

[1] Dietrich Bonhoeffer, *The Cost of Discipleship* (New York: The Macmillan Co.; paperback ed., 1963), p. 129.

them. They took me outside where we could see the distant view. Pointing to a sail boat on the water the wife said: "Do you see that boat? Well, that is our God! And do you see those mountains behind it?" — and of course I did — "Well, that is where we get our inspiration!" Christianity, to this couple, was only a barrier to their way of living. They seemed to be making out fine without it.

On another occasion, in Alaska, while taking a census for the church, I came to one man and proceeded with the usual questions. Immediately he began his cynicism: "I came to Alaska to get away from religious hounds!" — and he had his own dogs for defense of that commitment. He really meant business as he reached for his shotgun and fondled the latch on the door. I meant business, too, in my concerted attempt to beat his dogs to the gate.

In an age that seems to be espousing a pagan ethic and surviving, it is hardly understandable why Christianity is necessary at all. But with a pagan ethic there eventually comes a pagan downgrade. This has been true in every era. As a contemporary trend in world crises looms before us it proves that something more than pagan is needed. The world, left to itself, without the redemptive influence of Christ, is left without a resource for survival. The New Testament leaves us the remarkable dictum: "In Him all things hold together." [2]

The Christian evangel who is indeed salt and light — a *solution* and *guide* for ailing civilization — will be a cardinal asset to any lasting coherence in the world. At least Christ banked on this principle and committed His faith and life to its cultivation. He spent His ministry with a motley band of fisher folk and common men attempting to salt them with fire.

If we can apprehend what Christ intended in His simile of "salt" and "light," we can more nearly understand what it is to which He calls the church.

[2] Colossians 1:17 (*The Modern Language New Testament*).

Christ was no organic chemist, nor was He an astronomical genius. He did not bother to explain the chemical components of common table salt. Nor did He give the genius of the natural laws governing light. But He knew the effects on human life of both salt and light. He could tell you that salt added zest and flavor to food. He could assure you that meat was preserved by salting. He could describe the healing, purifying effects salt had on open wounds. He could tell you that, for some peculiar reason, the human metabolism craved salt, indeed must have it to survive. [3] By simple observation alone He could conclude that salt is one of the most indispensable elements to human life — especially in His day, when preservatives, medicines, and substitutes were not available.

Christ knew, also, the simple effects of light on human life. This made it another indispensable element. He knew that the processes of seeing were not geared for abject darkness. To function properly, the eyes needed the light. Christ had seen the sunken eyes of lepers inflamed with *iritis* and recalcitrant to the sunlight, enough to know that the lack of light had a tremendous bearing even on their physical appearance.

In our own time, scientists have discovered, trapped in darkened ocean caves, fish that have no eyes. In the darkness, their eyes were non-essential. In response, nature intervened, and subsequent generations of fish were born without eyes. Verification came in the scientific control data when the captured fish, reared a few generations in the light, took recourse by being spawned with eyes.

Christ had still other familiar proof of the indispensability of light to all of life. He knew that grass and herbs and berries did not flourish in the shade. He knew the warmth of the sun, and the chill of the night when the sun receded behind the horizon. He knew the deadening effect of winter (when the sun is most distant) on vegetation and the animal

---

3 Salt contains elements known as *ions*, or electrically charged atoms, which are indispensable to the nerve cells of the body.

world which endured it. By simple observation, again, He could conclude that light was a most indispensable element of life. Is it happenstance then that He should say: "I am the light of the world: he that followeth me . . . shall have the *light of life*"? [4]

By His simile, then, Christ was saying in effect that His followers were indispensable to life. Out of this kind of people He would forge a community bent on captivating the imagination and heart of the world. Indeed, history is replete with illustrations of the Christian essential. Radiant believers have added zest and flavor to life. They have shown healing and preserving qualities. And they have influenced a new pattern of living. Eventually they forced the hand of the Roman Empire with their power of penetration and their exciting wholeness.

This indispensable quality dwindled when Christianity emerged as victor of the Roman conquest. Like aging wine, instead of maintaining a salient fermentation, it settled on its leas. Christ's simile became commonplace and Christianity began to lose its effectiveness. However, Christ had forewarned that salt could lose its saltiness. The implication was that the church could lose its wholeness.

Salt, to be salt, must maintain its two-fold compound — sodium and chloride. In so doing it becomes more than the sum total of its qualifying parts; otherwise, it would have damaging effects. The chemical components of salt may each become dangerous if separated.

Sodium, on the one hand, is a highly active substance. Under certain conditions it becomes an *explosive*. Combined with water, sodium produces hydrogen gas and an intensity of heat that could easily detonate the gas as it is released. In a casual conversation I was explaining this to a friend. He responded: "This must be why you hear of salt mines blowing up when water has leaked into them." Such an observation had never occurred to me, but he was correct.

[4] John 8:12 (k.j.v.). Italics are mine.

Chloride, on the other hand, being composed of chlorine and some form of metal, can be highly *poisonous,* especially when combined with lead and mercurous chloride. By a process known as *electrolysis,* deadly chlorine gas is extracted from a solution of salt water. The residue is sodium hydroxide which serves as a base for neutralizing hydrochloric acid. The product of this final procedure is common table salt. Thus, two elements, one an explosive, the other, a poison, combined in a wholeness become a very harmless, most indispensable necessity of life — common table salt. But the wholeness must be maintained at all cost. If it loses its wholeness, it loses also its properties to penetrate, to heal, to flavor, to preserve. When it does not *act* as salt, it loses its right to be *called* salt.

Analogies, of course, break down when carried too far. For this reason we would not have Christ saying more than He said. He may not have explained the components of salt, but He certainly understood its acting properties. Because He did, He also knew what He wanted His followers to be when He implored them to be the "salt of the earth." When the church loses its properties to be "salt" — that silent, pervasive, penetrating force working its way into the thoughts of men, to change, to flavor, to preserve life — then it loses its right to be called Christ's church. When it loses its qualifying parts, its dynamic properties, its wholeness, it easily becomes a power that damages or a force that poisons.

The church is called to be salt because it is called to be a *whole people* to save a *fragmented world.* "Can you be dedicated to Missions and not to personal wholeness?" That is what I asked one person who related to me that if only she and her husband could be accepted by a Mission Board, most of their anxieties would be alleviated. Yet in the group she related many dissatisfactions and problems that were besetting their family life. Here was the mistaken idea that a spiritual ministry could be promulgated without a struggle for personal wholeness. It was the sure sign of a mechanistic escape into "religion" without "reality." There can be no discrepancy, however, between being *missionary* and being *real.* The pursuit of reality and wholeness is not necessarily bound up in the pursuit of that which will seemingly make us happy.

In fact, in the case of this couple their obsession was simply compounding the problem. Contrary to what some might have advised, I cautiously suggested that maybe what the family needed at this point was to stop pushing so hard toward the mission field, as they had been doing for the past five years; then to just get away for a period in which they could dedicate themselves to strengthening their inner life and building the family complex. Our debilitating anxieties are better alleviated through mature surrender and love to one another. Then, if ever, we are ready for the mission field. Until then, *we* are the mission field.

There must be some amount of winsome, spiritual magnetism in the church's healthiness if it is to pour its influence on the world. A fault with modern evangelism is that it often has nothing to give once it arrives at its destination. It has assumed the role of penetration, using all sorts of repugnant implementation, without much substantial, enticing beauty. Moralism has been among the worst. Many well-meaning young evangels have stepped to the door of reputable folk and have taken the household as a black tempest would a palm tree. Startled and subdued, the unknowing victims then have been told that the Gospel of Jesus Christ is "free" to all — quite a contrast in disposition. In my early ministry I could well have been numbered among the moralists. I soon learned by experience, however, that there was little winsomeness in that approach and absolutely no love at all.

When I went to one church as pastor, a kind lady drew me aside and said: "I hope you won't be like many ministers who have come. My husband has been rubbed the wrong way by arm-twisting evangelists. He has cautioned me that the next one will be booted out the front door."

I went to meet this gentleman with caution under my collar because I didn't want to generate coals under his.

In the course of this first conversation and many that were to follow over the years, I found a genuine likableness in this man. We became fast friends and are until this day. I never "pressured" him one way or the other regarding his relationship to Christ. There were times when I shared something of my own background regarding my faith. There were times, too, when our discussions got a little heated because each of us felt so strongly about certain issues — but we never exploited one another. I invited him to church *one* time and told him then that he would just have to know that he was welcome because I would never play the game of coaxing him to come. I worked at his job with him some, ate at his table and stayed in his home as a guest. His wife later told me that I was the only minister he had ever invited to stay overnight. When I moved from the community to another church, he was the first to look me up among all the friends I had left behind. Although he had come to church only one time while I was there, he later began taking his family to a church in a near-by city. I learned from this experience what my professor meant when he told us that we ought to be "kind rebels." "Above all else," he taught us, "the Christian should be a gentleman."

Perhaps some enticing beauty is what our Christianity needs. Christian penetration may be altogether valid, but it must not be uncouth. We have missed the most valuable insight into "the salt of the earth" if we miss the appropriateness of spiritual magnetism. We have learned in our scientific age that salt does more than penetrate; it *draws*. The simple process called "osmosis" is an illustration in point. In science class we placed a thin membrane in a pan as a divider separating sugar water and salt water subsequently poured into the container. Soon the salt water had drawn the sugar through the thin membrane leaving in one side of the pan a residue of clear water. On another occasion I once asked a lady for her secret of cooking juicy roasts for which she was quite famous among her family and friends. She told me that she salted the meat only after it was nearly done. The salt, if placed on the meat too early, she informed me, would draw all the natural juices from the meat leaving it dry. Perhaps from this modern insight we can learn a new wisdom for the church as the "salt of the earth." The Christian church, if it is actually "salt," will not have to go out and penetrate society by perfunctory effort; it will draw society quite winsomely.

This interpretation is not totally foreign to Christ's intent in His simile. As He walked and lived among people He drew them to Himself. His life was as much *magnetic* as it was *penetrating*. His death would guarantee that such magnetism would persist among His followers. Once toward the end of Christ's ministry, some Greeks came to Philip with the appeal: "Sir, we would see Jesus." Informed of this request, Christ recognized in it the heart-cry of the human race. How would He answer this cry? Knowing that He was not long with them He turned to His disciples and said: "The time has come for the Son of man to be glorified *and* exalted. I assure you . . . unless a grain of wheat falls into the earth and dies, it remains [just one grain; never becomes more but lives] by itself alone. But if it dies, it produces many others *and* yields a rich harvest." [5] In the Cross Christ no longer remains a solitary kernel. He reproduces His spirit and life in the hearts of His followers. Out of this jolting event is to come a great "harvest" of men and women who in turn will serve as "saviors" to the world — to point men to the Real Savior. As He dies, He lays the tools of evangelism at the foot of the Cross.

One of the "tools" that Christ would leave His followers is "personal magnetism." After Christ had answered Philip and the others He said: "And I, if I be lifted up from the earth, will draw all men unto me." [6] How? The same magnetic, drawing power, like faggots aflame, would burn it-

[5] John 12:23, 24 (Amplified).
[6] John 12:32 (k.j.v.).

self into the character of His people. Through them He meant to *attract* the world to the Gospel and to life.

Society must envision God through what Woodrow Wilson called "the atmospheric pressure of Christianity." Penetration, in other words, must be endemic to the character of Christianity. Evangelism is no seasonal garb to be modeled pretentiously. The early Christians did not go about "peddling" or "hawking" Jesus Christ. By their own muscular spirit under Christ they allured and abated pagan impugnity. They perfumed the air, in a measure, with a demonstration of Christ's very likeness. The chief asset in Paul's mind was to be made "the fragrance of Christ to God," serving as "a living perfume that leads to life" for an unbelieving world. [7] What a symbol for unbridled permeation — "perfume"! Men catch its aroma merely by breathing.

Somehow the church has missed Paul's gesture and has conjured a strained out-reach of its own. Methodology has become the controlling wisdom to the point of the ridiculous. The greatest injunction of Christ against patent unreality was His dislike of religious people "advertising" their faith, parading their commitment. Quite revealing, however, is the fact that sign-post Christianity has never worked. It is simply another way of peddling the Gospel. You just do not "advertise" God! The signs, for instance, that churches place on the highways to caution or inform the public regarding God, are sometimes as humorous as they are tragic. One that has occurred again and again is the little moralism: "Get right with God!" Upon that moralistic demand, are people going to rush right up to claim God? Probably not. Another overly-used sign is that of a Scripture reference: "I am the way, the truth, and the life." There is nothing wrong with letting the world in on the Scripture; but the subtlety with which it is passed on is often vain. One such sign depicting Christ as "the way, the truth, and the life," drew more curious attention to the ones who placed it there than to the One

[7] 2 Corinthians 2:15, 16 (C. B. Wms.).

about whom it spoke. The paint was peeling badly, its letters were barely visible and the entire framing had all but fallen to the ground. Yet here in the mind of some saintly artisan was the symbol, the advertisement supposedly, of One who is indeed the "Life." All that remains in your mind as you drive on down the highway is the gesture that somewhere God's people must be going out of the painting business. There is little recognition of a *living* Christ in the unkempt, *fading* work of men.

Living Christianity is no longer indispensable when it must resort to gimmicks and trivia to win its world. This is precisely what Nat Tracy meant when he wrote: "the first 250 years of Christianity were marked with the Church's power to penetrate and transform a pagan society. This was done by its own robust spiritual health in a spirit of spontaneity and naturalness. When the Church had to organize special efforts to win its world, it therein betrayed its loss of spiritual vigor."[8]

X Finally, when the church is in spiritual health, or when the world can sense that it is at least genuinely in pursuit of health, then it may begin to serve as *light;* then it no longer has to conjure a strained out-reach. This does not mean that the Christian life will become effortless and determined. It will become all the more "visible" to demonstrate how part of the divine family lives. But it will shine under discipline, not out of craftiness and pretense — and certainly not become exploitative. In this way life catches a glimpse of a radiant character. The big problem comes when the church cannot thus demonstrate itself in life, when it cannot actually be the "light of life" for others in a winsome way.

As is the case of "salt," light to be light must maintain its properties to be light. Those properties are twofold: "to shine" and "to warm." The Apostle John said that Christ was the "Light" and that the darkness in the world could

[8] Tracy, "Conference on Spiritual Renewal," (Oct. 21, 22, 1966), No. 20, p. 4.

not put it out. Might it be that in the church God is preparing such men of light that they will not be swallowed up
in the darkness but will instead lighten the way for those
who lurk in the shadows — the lonely, the disconsolate, the
empty, the oppressed?

Being merely visible, however, is not necessarily the total
answer. Some of us, sorrowfully, have little light because
we have little heat. Everyone knows that it requires heat to
produce light. Probably the starting point, then, in becoming the "light of life" for men, is for the church first to offer
the world a new kind of personal *warmth*.

Chapter 10

A Christian Availability

> In this uniform no one will
> recognize the livery of people
> who are available, ready to do
> some down-to-earth labor.
> — *J. C. Hoekendijk*

During my college days in Texas, I met a remarkable student whose witness for Christ left me seriously questioning my own. Most college students, who are Christians, can talk in a lively way about their faith. I, for one, could drum up a rather exalted story of my own commitment. For those of us who liked to talk, however, there was never much explosion. Then we met Johnny Gayle. He was volatile in a very simple way. When most of the preachers on campus were secretly dreaming of becoming the next "Billy Graham," of surpassing William Carey or David Livingstone, or prating their vocal cords in mock sermonizing behind closed doors, Johnny Gayle was doing a rather thankless service for underprivileged kids of the city.

Every Friday afternoon, without fail, one could find five or six boys following Johnny into the dormitory. As they entered, it was obvious by their dress and appearance that they were youngsters from the "other side of the tracks." Later, I had a chance to visit the area where these boys lived. I saw disease and poverty, grime and rat-infested shacks made of adobe and cardboard. A very noticeable thing happened each Friday with these boys from that district. They entered the dormitory as ragamuffins and came out immaculately clean, wearing freshly ironed clothing, and smiling beneath long, but neatly combed hair. Then one could generally see Johnny taking them out for a hamburger or for some other activity. The striking note was that throughout the week, and especially on Fridays, Johnny made himself *available* to these boys.

At that time I was practicing some amateur barbering. By looking in the mirror, I had learned how to trim my own flat-top between regular haircuts. Students, who soon learned of my "trade" (with a detriment to my study time) beat a path to my door when they had no money for a haircut. One day the person who came to my door was Johnny himself. But he didn't want a haircut. Not for himself at least.

The conversation was immediately a little more other-centered. Johnny told me of his interest in the underprivileged children and explained to me his Friday afternoon ministry to them. The ministry was sponsored by a group on the campus known as the "Mission Band." He, of all the participants, really had his heart in the ministry and often was the only male ally to these young boys. He explained how some of the girls on campus managed each week to keep a change of clothes washed and ironed for the boys. Johnny would bring the boys into the dormitory and line them up in the shower room. From that time he proceeded to restore their appearance and their self-image. Now he was asking me: "Would you consent to cutting their hair from time to time?" Just like that! Simply, without fanfare or verbiage! "Are you interested?" Who could refuse? Here was a spirit blossoming with a warming, piercing sense of care. And here were boys whose hair had not been cut for months. Together they won my heart.

In the months ahead, with the croppings taken from these young heads, I could have braided a rope that might have reached from my third story room to the ground below. Time will not soon rob my memory of one little red-haired, freckle-faced boy who was brought to me for a haircut. An attempt to comb his hair, matted with everything from dirt to dead bugs, was futile. We coaxed him to the shower for a shampoo; then the cutting began. When the ordeal was over, a princely child stood before us. As he looked into the mirror, I recall, he could not believe the image. Neither could we. The expression on his face was so pleasing that we feared we had an angel on our hands.

In all the years since then, I have not seen another ministry so redemptive to the personal self-image. Nor have I seen any greater exercise of "Christian availability" than was demonstrated by this remarkable student. Because of his impressive spirit, I spent my weekends, before my first college pastorate, sharing Christ in the slum district. I had no money for its poor, and as I look back, not nearly enough love; but my own cup was running over with a satisfaction of meaning. I could understand much more appreciatively the heartbeat of Jesus Christ.

> There stands His feet among the poor and orphaned lot,
> And breaks the course of aimless men forgot;
> There rests His feet, beneath which no man's humble
> bow can plumb,
> And walks He there in clothes and ware of humble
> folk and blind;
> There strides He abreast His world, with clarion call
> and open grace,
> And keeps His company with the companionless of the
> race. [1]

The early Christians, as we observed in the previous chapter, were "indispensable" to their generation. They were so, not wholly because they intended to be but because Christ had produced in them this remarkable feature of "availability." Among them, Philip instantly comes to mind. He was one of the "Seven" (deacons) selected by the early community to dispense financial aid to certain widows who

[1] By the author.

were being neglected. [2] When the church began to flee the Persecution, Philip wound up preaching and ministering to the people in Samaria. He was simply being available when the Spirit of God told him to leave this "tremendous revival meeting" in Samaria to minister to one lone soul in the desert — the Ethiopian eunuch. The Scriptures then relate how he was borne away by the Spirit and put down at Ashdod. From Ashdod he traveled fifty-five miles on foot up the coastline to Caesarea. There he remained, and we hear nothing more of Philip until twenty years later when he is visited by Paul and his missionary companions. [3] What is so great about being a forgotten man? Just this: Philip had made himself available to some forgotten people — the Samaritans! If that is all Christ wanted him for, that was enough. He may be known forever as the first man to have broken out of the arrogant provincialism of Judaism.

All who were serious about their common calling as Christians were certainly part of what the New Testament calls the *diakonia*. This Greek word, in its verb form, means "to serve," or "to minister." During the early Christian era the word carried the secular identity of "waiting on tables." It became the symbol which portrays a *readiness* to serve. Once when a dispute arose between the disciples over who was the "greatest" among them, Christ said to them:

> The kings of the Gentiles exercise lordship over them; and those in authority over them are called benefactors. But not so with you; rather let the greatest among you become as the youngest, and the leader as one who serves (*diakonia*). For which is the greater, one who sits at table, or one who serves (*diakonia*)? Is it not the one who sits at table? But I am among you as one who serves (*diakonia*). [4]

In its masculine form (*diakonos*), the word for service has been popularly transliterated into anglican as "deacon"

[2] Acts 6:5.
[3] Acts 21:8.
[4] Luke 22:25-27 (R.S.V.). Parentheses explanatory.

but it meant far more than what is involved in its current connotation. Rather than a program of administration or a clerical office, the diaconate at first was an attitude, a posture of dexterity toward those in need. It became the Christian symbol of caring love.

In the early community the usage of this terminology was first attributed to the ministry of the "Seven" who were selected from the brotherhood as an emergency task-force. There is no verification in the New Testament, however, that this status continued *officially* when the emergency was past. The next crisis would call upon other "available" participants suitable to the need. The church would ordain them by the supportive, affirmative sign of the "laying on of hands," and deploy them as "servants of the brotherhood." [5]

What was at first meant to be a thorough-going "Christian availability" in ministry, reached the status of an officialized deaconship only in the later apostolic church. Although Paul used the word in the official sense, he did not create such an office. He merely exercised his interpretation in light of what had become of the *diakonia* by A.D. 62. Even then it did not have the smell of the cloister, or the dullness of so many committee-men, but the smell of the street and the aliveness of a spirited servanthood.

One stressing caricature in history is that every movement, when it has lasted, has eventually become institutionalized, officialized. This is a damaging trend for power's sake, because invariably life gives way to the empty shell. Christianity, in handing out credentials to the commonly called, began parceling out *attitudes* and replacing them with *badges*. However, the badge has never carried the spiritual force that inner attitudes and character hold.

This New Testament exemplar of availability has been even more grossly confused in the modern church. Perhaps many do not know that the word "deacon" has been entered

[5] W. O. Carver, "Introduction," *What Is the Church,* ed. by Duke K. McCall (Nashville, Tenn.: Broadman Press, 1958), p. 4.

in the English dictionary as a slang word. It carries a listing of such synonyms as to "adulterate," to "sophisticate," and to "meddle." Have we selected the improper word for describing the work of servants? Or is it prophetic for our time? Is it merely a cultural blunder of contemporary linguists? Or did the word come on as a colloquialism to describe a general downward trend in the deaconship? Whatever the word has come to mean, "the history of the diaconate can be written as the account of the ever-repeating attempt to detract from the original." [6]

Hoekendijk observes that the "diaconate" originally meant a readiness to live in *solidarity* and *service* with the needy of this world. For all intents, the original was a ministry of *help;* today, on the other hand, it is a confining and often sterile performance within the four walls of the meeting house. The deacon is too often the boutonniere-clad man who passes the collection plate, serves as a "checks and balance" man for the proper functioning of the minister, and oversees the administrative matters. Once a servant on street level, he has now become a clericalized component part of an intricate duty-bound machine. He has become an assistant on the inside, well-clothed and set apart. Suited for performance, he thus awaits his perfunctory role from meeting to meeting. "In this uniform no one will recognize the livery of people who are available, ready to do some down-to-earth labor." [7]

How do we go from modern consequences to pristine antecedent? Can there be a return to the original diaconate as "Christian availability"? Answers, of course, are always difficult; suggestions, however, are always easy. What we are searching for, remember, is a spirit, an attitude. This spirit obviously needs awakening, whether through a diaconate formed as a permanent body or as an intermittent task-force commissioned fluidly as the need arises. To me, the latter seems to be the more appropriate safeguard; for the

---

[6] J. C. Hoekendijk, *The Church Inside Out,* p. 148.
[7] *Ibid.*

"spirit" seems better kept when the "badge" is not so apparent.

Recently I was called upon by a Sunday school leader to teach the sixteenth chapter of *Romans* to a group in the college department. The chapter speaks of Phoebe the "deaconess" who had made herself available for some down-to-earth Christian business. Although the passage is partly shrouded in mystery, it is clear that Phoebe was on her way from the church at Cenchreae to the church at Rome. One is left to wonder just what Phoebe intended to do in behalf of the house-church community of Cenchreae, or, in fact, for Rome. The striking note is that she had been "available" before. Paul commends her to Rome as a "servant" of the church at Cenchreae, as a person who had already "stood by" many, including himself. There is no way of knowing whether Phoebe was a badge-wearing deaconess, but the spirit of *diakonia* is there.

That women will begin to wear the badge of deaconship with any amount of profundity is not likely in our day. Such has been a much debated issue. Rather than arguing the trivial, however, why not let all be deacons? What appears more plausible is for the church to drop its silver-star service in lieu of a more crisis-centered ministry. In such liberating atmosphere the members, under the imperative demands of truth and their own personal conscience, feel infinitely more significant.

Put to the Sunday school class, therefore, was this hypothetical suggestion: An imminent crisis is threatening an individual, or a family, or a business, or a sister church, or an entire city. Does it matter what crisis — illness, destitution, marital trouble, bankruptcy, flood or fire? The pastor, accordingly, seeks available members who have a special gift for whatever the task. These are brought before the church, approved in conduct and spirit, and offered as a corporate commitment-in-reply. The church in silent worship prays for those selected, affirming their dedication. Finally, in a gesture of full support, the church bids them

Godspeed by the "laying on of hands." This does not mean, in the least, that the individual needs the sanction of the church to do some prime labor in the world; but neither does it alter the fact that a service of this nature would be deeply moving. As an army marching under orders, God's people move out in Christ's name. The whole church is thus made available and sensitive, whether in actual ministry or in spiritual backing. Everyone now *belongs*. No one wears the badge. Once again, the church descends to the street where it becomes useful, needed.

This alternative is an unpopular intimation, but then it always has been. It was unpopular when Jesus, Himself a "deacon," went public without token. His only badge was a cry — "Come unto me all ye that labor and are heavy laden, and I will give you rest." We remember this cry as the soliloquy of the most available being in the universe — Jesus Christ. This cry was His own inner agreement with the Father that readiness to serve is the only answer to the burden of the race. Out of the dry ground of Israel's arrogant favoritism He came, quietly and with the touch of other-centered utility, assuringly and with an undying spirit of availability to the human race. Somehow we keep hearing His penetrating resonance: "I am among you as one who serves." Again he said, "The Son of Man did not come to be served (*diakonia*), but to serve (*diakonia*), and to give his life a ransom for many." [8]

Perhaps "availability" is the answer, because our cold world would warm to the moral character of more "deacons" like Jesus Christ.

---

[8] Mark 10:45 (Personal Translation). Parentheses explanatory.

Chapter 11

Dreaming Innocence

> "Where there is no vision, the
> people perish."
> — Proverbs 29:18 (K.J.V.)

Karl Marx said to his wife as he dreamed up the philosophy of Dialectical Materialism (popularly called "Communism"): "If we can but weld our souls together, then with contempt shall I fling my glove in the world's face, then shall I stride through the wreckage a creator." Within the gamut of a little over one hundred years, Communism has assumed control over the minds of two-thirds of the world's population. No one would have thought that a dream could be so explosive.

The only antidote for redressing the wrongs created by this destructive, totalitarian philosophy, is that of a brand of Christianity that out-dreams the spirit of Communism. The hierarchy of values must be nobler than the products of Dialectical Materialism. Christianity must be inwardly impelled to dream in unity and to dream well. The small group within the ranks of Christianity, from which Communism adapted its "cell bloc," must afford the atmosphere for dreaming the valuable dreams.

Everyone knows the rigor with which other great men have dreamed and the accomplishments each has made in his generation. Franklin D. Roosevelt spurred a buckling society with the words: "Each age is a dream that is dying or one that is coming to birth." Sir Winston Churchill wrote:

135

"The empires of the future are the empires of the mind."
Within more recent history, the dictum of the late Senator
Robert F. Kennedy burns within us: "Some men see things
as they are and ask why they are so. Let us dream of what
could be and ask 'why not?' " The church today might take
to heart the aspiring resonance of yesterday's voices. Indeed,
"why not?" Everyone today is champing at the bit to get on
with the "impossible dream."

Let me point out then in this chapter three principles for
dreaming these — what at first may appear to be — "impossible dreams."

First, *dreaming may be one form of an individual's prayer
life and devotion to God.* The great dreams and longings of
the heart openly expressed may at times be the only form
of dialogue with God. It does not matter how innocent,
simple, halting or inarticulate those aspirations may be. God
seems to hear and answer the open heart that dreams boldly
with abandonment those really unutterable, inexpressible
yearnings. I have a feeling that God chuckles at our "dreaming innocence." We do not even know for what we pray at
times. We certainly do not know what God has in store for
us. We may be crying and struggling, while God may be
smiling — because He knows. Sometimes, therefore, it may
be best merely to dream and let God be the Interpreter. "The
Spirit himself intercedes for us with sighs too deep for
words." [1]

The personal always seems best to express one's meanings.
I recall quite vividly how I felt that Christmas when I returned home from college as a first-semester sophomore.
The family economy was in no shape to be deployed indulgently. There were five children in our family, three of
whom were still at home — no small task for even the hardest
working of breadwinners. Going back to college a second
term meant the payment of another tuition. To meet this
demand my father had worked hard and, in spite of other
imposing claims, the money would come — of that I was

[1] Romans 8:26 (r.s.v.).

certain. And the money did come as predicted. But I was not content to stand by idly with upturned palms (although they were not always so, being accustomed, as it were, to a daily shriveling in the college cafeteria dish-water!). What I was earning there weekly, however, was a mere pittance in comparison to a lusty college bill.

Before I returned to college that second term, the strongest of drives clutched me at dead-center. For once in my life I wanted to sever the economic umbilical cord that would free my parents to breathe in repose. An attempt at financial independence was indispensable to my own emotional welfare. I knew it, and God knew it even better. So, with the joy and courage that only a Turk in the wine cellar would dare to ventilate, I specified, with architectural accuracy, my pipe-dream to God. (Today I wouldn't touch that kind of dictation with a rosary, much less a ten-foot pole.) Nonetheless, I prayed, I dreamed — asking God for a church to pastor near the college. Daily I dreamed my way into the pulpit. I virtually spent hours each day preparing sermons to a mock congregation. I was "changing the world" by proxy. I became bold; I felt in charge of my affairs. God was going to make me self-supporting.

When I returned to college, a few weeks passed and nothing happened. I solicited no church, and no church called. Dreaming continued until one day a letter came in the mail. It was from a rural church thirty miles from the college. They wanted me to "fill the pulpit" the following Sunday in view of a "call." At that point I could have "filled" anything; and what they didn't know is that God was already "calling." I met the engagement with excitement. The people there were "tuned in" and we "touched." Unknown to me, a pulpit committee from a neighboring village was attending the evening service. They proposed that I come to their church the following Sunday, and I accepted. God was "calling" again!

Following the evening benediction that second Sunday, I was requested to step outside the church while the people voted either to extend or refuse a "call." When I stepped into the church yard I was aghast. There standing before me was the pulpit committee from the other church! They had also extended to me a unanimous call and had come to get my reply. Hardly three minutes had passed when the church door opened behind me, and the pulpit committee chairman stepped from inside, walked to where we were standing and said: "Son, the church has just extended a unanimous call. Would you care to step inside and give us your answer?" What I did not know was that, because these two churches had "preaching" services only every other week (although they met each Sunday) they had often shared the same pastor over the years. I heartily accepted both calls. For the five years following, these people gave me a place to belong. My tenure there is priceless to this day. Needless to say, I didn't change the world, even a portion of it, but I learned gratefully that God honors "dreaming innocence."

I keep telling myself that because God loves us, He accommodates Himself to our dreaming innocence. His providence in our lives over and over tells us that He overhears our longings and answers our need.

I was nearing the end of my final semester in college and needed twenty-five dollars to complete my account. We were told that we would not be allowed to graduate until all outlying school debts were paid. I suppose that asking God outright for the money would not have been presumptuous, but I do not recall praying directly about the matter — probably because the deadline was not near enough.

During the course of the semester the college had scheduled its annual "Democracy-in-Action" week. Overnight it seems the faculty and student body became politicians and reformers on the American bandwagon. Renowned speakers such as General MacArthur and Charles Malik, among others, were flown in to lecture on Communism and the principles of American Democracy. Literary, art, and speaking contests were designed especially for the student to allow him a creative involvement during the week. One such contest for theology students was that of "sermon writing." The subject for the sermon had to be something directed toward the Communist threat in the world. Feverishly I entered the contest not knowing all that much about Communism. I finally settled on a title: "The World We Do Not Know — But Ought To Know," and went to work on the research.

I dreamed of taking the winner's wreath or whatever reward in the offing. I researched awhile and dreamed awhile. Soon I had accumulated so much material that I could have written five sermons — but I put it all into one.

The final day came for turning in the manuscript, anonymously marked of course, with only a number attached to it for identification by the student. I swear there was not a minute left when I plopped my "masterpiece" onto the professor's desk. The drudgery was over, but I retraced my steps every day. I even envisioned myself stepping up to the winner's platform on announcement day and receiving my award.

Announcement time came only a few days before Commencement. The awards were being distributed during a special chapel session. Perspiration dripped from my palms. Sluggishly the moments crept on until that special pause before the name — and my name was called. I could hardly keep back the tears as I proceeded to the stage and back again. As I slumped into my seat I took a cursory glance at the check in my hands — $25.00!

When the crowd began to disperse I could hardly make it to the registrar's office fast enough to pay my bill. From there I made my way to the student center where all my friends by this time had congregated. I faced the fanfare of handshakes and congratulations with a few tears streaming down my face. I recall a friend of mine, Noel Cowan (now a medical doctor), saying to me: "Why, you should be smiling!" That was certainly true enough — but he didn't know what I knew.

I am finding more and more that dreaming makes prayer life and devotion to God much more an adventure of faith. Perhaps this is what Paul had in mind when he challenged the Thessalonians to "pray without ceasing." [2]

Second, dreaming may arise out of the Christian community itself as the community dialogues together. No man accomplishes much by dreaming alone, for he is by nature first a dependent being and secondly a being capable of self-delusion. Every honorable dream attains its destiny tried in the fires. The lonely soul has no test for his dreams; he needs the dialogue of his brethren — and in the midst of his brethren, God attends. The great movements of the ages may have had their inception in the heart of some lone daysman, but only those men who have drawn around themselves others who have held affinity with their dreams and intents have ever accomplished their purposes. Marx's dream, in collaboration with his wife, is a case in point.

Jesus of Nazareth saw the truth in this principle. He gathered around Himself those who eventually dreamed His dreams. He sent twelve men into the world, not singly waging the destiny of their own insights and tactics, but in pairs for the necessary creative support in every engaging venture.

Paul, akin to Christ's strategy, ever saw the necessity of dreaming corporately with God's people everywhere. He had countless Christian communities pursuing objectives. He rooted them in spiritual ambition; and he cast his lot with their yearning. Let men dream in the plural, for this is the mortar that welds together "servant people" into *koinonia*. "Where there is no vision, the *people* perish." [3]

The Lay Training Center that I now direct in Christian Concern Foundation is actually a long-standing dream. It began about seven years ago in the minds of a fellowship of people who were searching their hearts for an innovative ministry in the church. What stimulated our concern was

[2] 1 Thessalonians 5:17 (k.j.v.).
[3] Proverbs 29:18 (k.j.v.). Italics are mine.

the growing interest in "renewal" brought on by some exciting ministries taking place in the Church of the Saviour in Washington, D.C.

During a week-long lay meeting in our fellowship, emotions ran high as we shared our visions together. We talked of every kind of ministry conceivable. One came to the fore that stimulated us all — a school of Christian living.

At that time, although I was part of the fellowship, I did not live in its city; so I was staying in the Traveler's Hotel — a sturdily built structure, but badly in need of repairs. I was spending many of the days in my room preparing radio messages which I was delivering each morning. All through the week, "School of Christian Living" oscillated in my mind. As this new idea peppered my thoughts I became restless. Suddenly, out of the clear blue, it struck me! "This hotel! Sure, it's up for sale! Why not!" Instantly I set to work putting on paper aspects of such a ministry. In a while I had typed two pages of material, along with a proposal to the fellowship. I could hardly wait to look into its possibilities for materializing.

The realtor had a $30,000 price tag on the hotel — certainly more money than our fellowship had seen in all our life spans combined. The manager took me on a tour of the building and by the time we had returned to the lobby I had mentally changed every nook and cranny and had visualized a Christian center in full operation.

With this information, my "clear blue" dream moved me to look for my "true blue" friend in the ministry, Creath Davis, who at this time was pastor among the fellowship. [4] We called together three men of the fellowship and went to the hotel. The tour was on again, and every nook and cranny received another mental coat of paint. Before nightfall the following day we were ready to present our fantasy to the entire church. From this point, you know what happened. We didn't buy the hotel; for who had $30,000? Two years

[4] Creath Davis is presently Executive Director of Christian Concern Foundation, Dallas, Texas.

ago the hotel was purchased by the government and converted into housing for the aged. Every time some of us in the fellowship pass by the building together, someone is always sure to quip: "Well, there's Robert's hotel!"

The dream didn't die. We gave it to God, and I filed my documents away for safe keeping.

This brings me to my third and final point. *Dreams must be given away or die a meaningless death.* Approximately a year and a half ago, God gave us back our dream for a "School of Christian Living" — in a different setting and in a different form, but the same dream no less. Perhaps before, it was the wrong place and the wrong time; surely, it wasn't because God needed time to catch up with us.

For many years Creath and I have felt that God wanted us in some kind of ministry together. In August of 1970, we were talking long distance on the telephone and our dream took on an aura of resurrection. This was on Thursday. On the weekend we spent time at Kaleo Lodge on retreat together. Under much excitement we shared our dream with a few board members of the Foundation. In the few days that followed, the board voted to open the door to the venture if we could raise my salary. We couldn't, but God did, and the Lay Training Center became a reality. God had given new birth to a seven-year-old dream. He has a way of working miracles you know! And who knows but what this dream may be only the threshold to an even greater? When dreams are God-given and Christ-oriented, they are always open-ended.

To keep dreams from becoming self-absorbing we must cut the ropes and give them away. We must share them with one another, to be sure, but we must give them into the hands of God at all cost. "The final test of the true maturity and completely integrated quality of a dream is one's willingness to give it away." [5]

For this reason alone, "Dreaming Innocence" may be faith

[5] Glenn Clark, *I Will Lift Up Mine Eyes* (New York: Harper & Brothers, 1937), p. 47.

or it may be pusillanimity. When one gives his dreams to God, with human welfare in view, that is faith — and faith is freeing. When he directs his dreams away from God, away from human beneficence, that is pusillanimity — sheer self-absorbing ignorance. There is no greater bondage.

This book itself is becoming the product of a dream given away. Two years ago on a farm in a little Texas community, I stood beneath a Post Oak tree and asked God for this book. Little did I know that God would give it to me so soon. But with each succeeding chapter I am made aware that this is not my book. I am in partnership with God because He took my dream. He looked it over; and when the time was ripe, He gave it back to me.

Everyone in the Christian community should have a dream. Age has no bearing on the matter. The promise of God is to those who know the presence of God's Spirit within. The prophet Joel said to Israel: "Your old men shall dream dreams, your young men shall see visions." [6] On the day of Pentecost Peter renewed the prophet's words to the "New Israel," the church. [7]

Someone has said: "The difference between an impractical dreamer and a man of vision is about two generations." Some of our dreams may be wild, too immature, even fanatical. They may seem too presumptuous; but dream them anyway! So long as we are dreaming we are reaching out beyond ourselves.

[6] Joel 2:28 (k.j.v.).
[7] Acts 2:17.

Chapter 12

A Ministry of Listening

> "If ever you were willing to listen, listen now!"
>
> — Matthew 11:15
> (Living New Testament)

The church must remain "in touch" with itself if it is to remain healthy, and "in touch" with the world if it is to be redemptive. We really need one anothers' ideas and support if our lives are to be constantly nourished and changed. The reason for this says John Lagemann, "is because man is an incomplete animal — to be real to himself he needs to be real to another. Our minds have to touch to stay alive." [1]

A living Christianity will produce a living world; but Christianity will become vibrant only as it begins to "listen."

The Bible speaks much about the "uncircumcised ear." To those knowing the intricacies of the Jewish rite of circumcision this was a boon to communication. These people understood the gesture to be talking about the insulated, insensitive ear. This is a valuable biblical principle because relationships cannot be maintained on monologue.

Monologue persists as we fail to listen to one another. Not to listen is the first injunction against the right to be heard. Our physical make-up is a close second. Someone has humorously explained it by saying that if God wanted us to

---

[1] John Kord Lagemann, "Conversation Can Nourish Your Life," *The Reader's Digest* (June, 1966), p. 132.

speak more than to listen He would have given us two mouths and one ear. Gratefully, the opposite is the case. The church has a right to speak — to itself and to the world — but only as it learns the art of listening.

First, then, the Christian community must listen to itself. By listening to people we assure their very existence. We give them a place within the human race as well as within the fellowship. We affirm them when we are interested in what they are saying. I have never seen the point borne out quite so vividly as in a moving experience during a former pastorate. As the men of the church sat in dialogue, one in the group shared his boyhood experience of running away from home. He had been orphaned early in life and was being reared by a rather caustic, overbearing grandfather. By his early teens the boy had taken all the scathing he could take. Almost in tears now, he shared his helmless plunge into "nowhere." Hopping trains, crossing dry fields, barbed wire fences, traveling without food or water, he wandered through the hot days of summer into the future, never to return home. The sites of his lodging at night, the men along the route who gave him work, food — the whole eerie picture came into play with our emotions. We understood. Or was it that we were able to *feel*, along with him, what he had encountered? We were listening to a man who knew what it meant to be a boy without roots, a boy without a place of warmth. He needed to share that story and we needed to listen. By so doing we gave him a place to belong. We gave him roots. Moreover, the encounter made us all aware that we were alive. The listening side of dialogue dispelled any element of self-doubt. Tournier has so aptly phrased it:

> We feel we exist in so far as others accept, respect, and welcome our existence, in so far as they prove it by listening to us, answering us and entering into dialogue with us.

> The essence of psychotherapy is the open-hearted talk, the expression of one's thoughts in the confidence of being really listened to and understood, entry into per-

sonal communication and receiving a response — in short, the living experience of dialogue.[2]

The Christian community at all cost must be *deeply sensitive* to the need some in the group have of talking out their feelings, whether of triumph or foreboding. This is to say that the members must *serve as "dialogical midwives."* They must help those in the group having trouble opening up the soul to give birth to their thoughts. Some "one" person must make it his ministry to get next to the heart-beat of the weak. He must be a person with a listening ear, who is tender and patient, but who also knows how to provoke response genuinely. To accept the human soul before you eventually bring down the defenses. You both become the richer for having been open to the tattered and often desperate, unsolaced needs of the man next to you. When this occurs the weak becomes strong and is made capable to bare his feelings to the group, knowing that he has support.

One day a person entered one of our Prayer Therapy groups. He recognized some deeply buried hostilities within himself. Apparently he did not know how to deal with them or how to vent them in a constructive and appropriate way. In correspondence with Dr. William R. Parker of the University of Redlands,[3] I came to understand more clearly why this person in our group had taken on such a passive approach in life and such a dominant resistance to reality. Part of his problem was his uncertainty of the group. His need to conceal found rationalization in a nebulous "escape into religion." Dr. Parker wrote:

> As long as he holds this within himself, he will remain passive, . . . and will further move away from his feelings of destructive emotions and will begin to try to find an identity in a "Jesus meek and mild," which is not all the story. Jesus was also capable of anger; He was virile, dynamic, and strong; and above all He was able

---

[2] Tournier, *A Place for You,* p. 106.

[3] Dr. Parker is also author of *Prayer Can Change Your Life* and originator of "Prayer Therapy."

to face the realities of His life. Because He was able to face the realities of His life, He did not judge or condemn.

.   .   .   .

It would seem to me to effectively help *B* - - - *R* - - - - - would be for him to expect his healing and rehabilitation to come through his honesty in the group . . . and in human relations. To assume that it may come through an historical figure, however wonderful, may be whistling in the dark. Once he has worked out his feelings in human relations, his relationship to the Divine then becomes meaningful and authentic.

The group opened its heart to this person, and in time he was sharing many of his emotional hang-ups uncoerced. It was in personal conferences first, however, that he began to confide in me many debilitating factors which, he assured me, had never been shared with anyone else.

Through this experience and others similar to it, I was made aware all over again of the need for people who will listen openly and sensitively to those struggling with crucial emotional problems. Christianity is basically the answer to our emotional conflicts but not unless it is embodied in people, who, under the auspices of Jesus Christ, are determined to care and who are humbly oriented to open up the soul to people in distress. I have been shamed many times as I have slowly, unconsciously closed my life to others and to their needs. But whenever the slightest ray of openness has been present in my life those are the times when relationships have been the most rewarding.

Second, the Christian community must listen to the world community. A "ministry of listening" incorporated within the dynamics of "community" will be the most pragmatic thing the church can do for its ministry to others. This ministry of listening will need both the equipping stage and the serving stage. The community may begin by listening to itself but it must end by listening to the world. At least two ways are available.

First, Thomas J. Mullen, in his study on the "equipping ministry," has revealed that some pastors have held what they have called "self-understanding" groups in their churches. In such groups the participants train themselves to listen intently to others and possibly sense the feelings behind their words. [4] This is the "equipping" stage which precedes actual service in the world.

There ought to be a "self-understanding" in the Christian Community that is unmatched anywhere else in the world. Self-understanding comes, however, only as people begin to listen to one another *seriously*. Without a deepening understanding at heart level, men do not *care*, for they cannot love what they do not understand. How we hear one another, therefore, will deeply affect our concern for one another. We will care markedly only as we come to *know* one another, not simply as we come to *know about* one another. Knowing, of course, comes by catching the heart-beat; and the "heart-beat" here is the kind, I surmise, that is felt more through the ears than through the pulse. We are not medics; we are persons who are under orders of Christ who said, "If ever you were willing to listen, listen now!"

Secondly, the dynamics of a listening ministry must range beyond the small group, beyond the walls of the church. Christianity has to hear more than the sounds within the cloister and attend mercifully to the heartache of human privation. Some persons are never listened to; they are living lives of quiet desperation, or are overvocal to conceal their loneliness. The elderly still need a place to belong, still need to be heard. Prisons house the discarded, the disconsolate. As long as they have a heart-beat they need to be heard. Hospitals are indeed sanctuaries of real need. The church has a "ministry of listening" captivated and waiting in these three arenas.

One day a man called me into his hospital room to sell me a car, but instead sold me his heart-beat. I did not think

---

[4] Thomas J. Mullen, *The Renewal of the Ministry* (New York: Abingdon Press, 1963), p. 99.

that man a weakling. I have not forgotten how it counts to listen to men in distress. About a month later, this same man was fatally shot by his estranged wife. Since that day I have tried to keep my ears open to the human heart-cry.

Have you ever watched young boys tossing restlessly at 3 a.m. behind the steel screens of a correctional school and later listened to their dejection over car-theft, murder and rape? Here are the alienated ones, the silent ones, needing a listening ear.

The same is true of men in prison — some of them devoted con-men, I am sure, but some deeply cut men, not in the least proud. While seated in the chaplain's office one day, awaiting a complaisant prisoner who was hoping for parole, I sensed the throbbing mixture of joy and pain that lurks behind prison walls. It made a tremendous impact on me as the prisoner came running full-speed down the long corridor toward me with outstretched hand, a smile on his face, and — I am sure — an anguished heart. As I listened, I sensed both the delight and the costliness of what it means to really care.

Through the ministry of listening, feeling, and placing yourself in the shoes of others, I am finding that you "become all men," or as Paul put it, "all things to all men."

Chapter 13

The Need for Creative Silence

> There is no substitute for
> intelligence; the nearest thing
> to it is silence.
>
> — *Anonymous*

Some of the most creative moments of my life have been
those times when I have sat in solitude on a hillside, or
ambled through a grove of towering pines listening to
nothing but my innermost thoughts. Again and again I
have found silence to be therapeutic. Delightfully it forces
a person into a state of repose and openness. In the silence,
God speaks! Motivation and renewal come in those moments
as a result of the least amount of obedience to that still,
small voice. Silence becomes creative because God com-
mands the best that is within me. I am called upon to leave
the doldrums, to reach out to life as it comes, to inaugurate
a dream, to summon courage for the next great enterprising
venture. I am purified best as the Spirit of God moves upon
the reservoir of my stillness — and I am powerless to resist.
"Again and again God makes a silence in our lives," writes
Weatherhead. "We listen to the birds at dawn, or the moan
of the sea at night. We gaze into the heart of a flower,
or watch the flaming sky at sunset. We spend an hour under

the quiet stars. The hush of the Infinite is upon us. We tell ourselves we will try again." [1]

If we are to know where we are going, we need first to know where we have been. Not only must we know where we have been but also the meaning of where we have been. To know meaningfully the nature of our present status calls for intelligent reflection and intelligent reflection calls for silence. Only then can we move creatively into life.

The early Christian community began its life in this fashion, behind closed doors. The faithful sat together soberly in a quaint room in Jerusalem waiting in silence and prayer for the empowering fullness of the Spirit. During those rather sullen moments something was needed, but no one knew just what. Only God could bring creativity into the silence.

Shortly, in obedience to something within him, Peter arose, took charge of the silence and moved the community into its first great task — the selection of an eye-witness to the events of Christ's Passion. This decision aspired for a new testimony to take the place of Judas in strengthening the support of believers against skepticism and speculation regarding the Resurrection. Christian *certainty* for the ages to come would grow out of this first silence.

Some of the best Christian orthodoxy arose from similar periods of quiet isolation. Examples are plentiful. The *gospel of John*, chapters 13-17, possibly the greatest of Christ's words on "spiritual unity," were given in the secretive halls of the Upper Room. The Sermon on the Mount, recognized generally as Christ's foremost communication of moral principles, was born in the stillness of a secluded hillside away from the noise of the crowd. The so-called "prison epistles" of Paul were written from the hush of solitary confinement. From an "isolated " house-church community the greatest of all spiritual world views, namely, the Christian world view, was passed on to a world lacking a winsome,

[1] Leslie D. Weatherhead, *The Transforming Friendship*, pp. 29-30.

liberating moral code. In these people, orthodoxy at its best became the silence of character stealing its way into the thoughts of men. Thus, on this common ledger of the church — epistles, gospels, life — the touch of silence had won its claim.

Has this refreshing breath of silence been missed by the modern church? Some feel that it has. There is the widespread feeling that the church has "talked itself to death." Some have thus concluded that the modern church, if it intends to influence an intelligent society, must come alive to the art of "creative silence." They feel relatively certain that what is not needed within the Christian community is a "fatal quietism," resulting in a passive role. Yet, what is needed even less, they say, is an "unbridled vocalism."

As much as the church is being warned today against the threat of hyper-activism, it is also being challenged against its empty, uncharted talk. Perhaps this is as it should be, for there are those who are assured by experience that silence is still golden and wisdom in speech is a necessary stop-gap between order and chaos. "There is no substitute for intelligence;" says an anonymous source, "the nearest thing to it is silence." Somewhere Robert Louis Stevenson wrote: "It was his gift to be fluent on anything or nothing."

The general opinion of thoughtful Christians is that this kind of *fluency* must not happen to the Christian witness. Life is choked to death under such fluency. Even the nervous system cannot thrive on monological noise. A relentless preoccupation with religious chatter in the church is nothing short of spiritual death. The only alternative, therefore, is a silence that breeds a forging, creative spirit. The new, emerging church, to be relevant to its own human need, as well as to reach out to an affluent society, must learn the appropriateness of creative silence. The inevitable question is "How?"

First, the church is sometimes "forced" into silence by defeat. This may not be a sound approach in learning what the church must learn, but it may put its thinking mechanism into gear. Our "victorious talk" in the church (when there is not much real victory) soon brings us to an embarrassing idleness. When the world does not respond, we never think to check our decibel level. Occasionally we may be *out-talking* our integrity of *action,* too loud for the sensitive ear. We may be perfectly willing to parade our virtues in talk only. We may not be quite so willing to brandish our true colors when occasional "slips of the tongue" prove fatal. Once we become seasoned by honesty — in our *stewardship* as well as our *talk* — then silence no longer has to be resignation in defeat. Silence was never meant to be a "gag" for Christians defeated by their own lack of integrity. When integrity can seep through the church's talkativeness, its eloquence, rather than menacing, may become an added boon to its honor.

The same principle holds true of our having to cope with the tiring voices of others. When the wind has been knocked out of our sails, we want to be alone. When we have to capitulate to some articulate soul who out-shines us in every way, we long for solitude. But woe to our longings for silence, we are too late — some "victorious person" is always on hand (well-meaning of course) to cheer us on. In need of sobering quietness for thinking through our situation, we must listen instead to the harangue of an insensitive victor. And the hardest thing in the world is to listen patiently to a winner when we ourselves have lost. We are silent nonetheless.

Thus sometimes, within the church or as individuals, the only road to silence is the back road of defeat. Apart from brooding, even that kind of silence can be creative and productive.

Secondly, we may be more "Christian" in our demand for personal growth and progress within the Christian community. Of all people, Christians have a way of making unrealistic demands on one another. We are sometimes worse than the Greek philosophers on Mars Hill, who traipsed through the colonades inquiring of the "latest thing going." If nothing is "happening" with us lately, if there is no "recent conquest," no "great news" to share with excitement, we invariably feel down, because most Christians who are "eternally up" expect us to be the same.

In his book, *A Second Touch,* Keith Miller clearly describes the problem of our overly affected approach to one another. He writes:

> In some segments of society in America, one is considered a shirker if he isn't driving himself to greater (larger) things. Especially in some groups of Christians, one has to have made a new discovery, led someone else to a deeper commitment, gone on a freedom ride, or read the latest book when he sees his old Christian friends — or he doesn't feel with it. [2]

Much of our "everlastingly-up-talk" is the result of our need to feel significant in the presence of others. To be on par sometimes means the tendency to exaggerate some of our most trivial experiences, talking of them like Wellington at Waterloo. Ministers themselves are a copious breed especially capable of stretching the longbow. Perhaps this is why the phrase "ministerially speaking" has humorously become an adverbial synonym for "exaggeration." Obviously, this is not strictly a ministerial *faux pas.* All of us are guilty of exaggeration; however, when exaggeration seems too blatant, we bolster our dignity in other ways. Feeling guilty or inconsequential we immediately begin to think up something to be famous for, because we all dream of a star-spangled history and disparage of an empty future. Christ and Christians, we think, demand a little more!

Such a philosophy of demand is the thinking of one who unceasingly has to "have something going," who cannot risk having "nothing" to share. The Christian community must

[2] Keith Miller, *A Second Touch* (Waco, Texas: Word Books, Inc., 1967), p. 55.

undercut this philosophy by allowing the participants to grow at their own pace under Christ: to be silent when they are silent, to be empty when they are empty, to be victorious when they are victorious. If Christ is alive in us, we are destined to grow; if He is not, we are destined to swell — and swelling has a tendency to go down when our Christian friends are not around to spur us on.

What many Christians do not recognize is that *the kingdom of God* grows at night, while men sleep. The kingdom of God is like the farmer who plants his seeds and then retires to his house to await their sprouting. He does not foolishly dig into the furrows each morning checking each seed for growth. The growth of the kingdom of God in man's experience is quite similar to this. Once the seed has been planted, no pampering, no persuading, no magic can accelerate its growth, and the "pushy" Christian only aggravates its maturity. The kingdom of God, like the grass, has a tendency to make its own soil as it finds its growing edge. Moralists who tend toward manipulation might learn a lesson about creative silence in Christian growth if only they would listen to the grass grow.

Man's ego knows no silence. For this reason discipline must be used in quieting self-conceit. Those who would cherish the value of creative silence must concede to a Christian modesty. *A third lesson, therefore, is this: that the participants in "community" cease their incessant drive for individual recognition.* We need a drive toward significance and meaning, but we do not need a new surge toward preeminence. We need to affirm one another honestly, give one another a place to belong genuinely, but we do not need to *deify* one another falsely.

Jealousy of place and personality within the Christian community is the last thing we need, but it is fast becoming a major problem, especially among these who are sounding the emerging note of "renewal." To out-do one's peers is in vogue: a more stately church building in the round, a bigger, better coffee-house ministry, a more elaborate retreat center, a more contemporary Christian beach house, and other, more commanding novelties are illustrations in point. Because *novelty*, in this instance, is the birthright of jealousy, one of the major pitfalls against which the emerging church must wage a ruthless warfare is that of internal aggrandizement — the proverbial pat on the back. Not only do we pat ourselves on the back too often but we also pat one another on the back too often — with false praise.

Too many of us have, or have had, what E. Stanley Jones (citing Bishop Quayle) called: *"ichus publendi"* — the "itch for publicity." Most of us Christians, he observes, had rather be the "light of the world" before being "the salt of the earth." We had rather be that effulgent, open declaration of success and glory than that silent, pervasive, unheralded participant. [3] Most of us know how to be those militant leaders out in front; few of us know how to be the unsummoned followers waiting behind in reserve.

Over-vocalism is the first sign of a person's drive for recognition. This is undoubtedly the wrong procedure when searching for a place to belong among one's peers. There have been times in my own life when I fear that I have "talked too much already" and suffered the consequences. Going through my initial Prayer Therapy group I learned that one of my chief inner fears was the fear of my own thoughts. The phobia had come by too many over-vocal experiences which left me frustrated. I was left with the battle of learning when to talk and when to keep silent. As a result, partly out of a sense of being "proper" and partly out of a sense of guilt, I set out to learn what it means to *participate in silence*. As I began to learn this lesson, I also discovered that I had been a poor listener, for in most instances I still had the urge to assert myself, however ill-destined or unproductive my words.

No one told me, but I soon learned that conferences and

[3] E Stanley Jones, *The Christ of the Mount: A Working Philosophy of Life* (New York: The Abingdon Press, 1931), p. 92.

small group sessions were not dedicated simply to sharing all the "great" things we were accomplishing. At least I recognized that this was a concerted attempt on my part to maintain my own sense of significance and coyly to aggrandize my own "true merit." As my effectiveness in relationships dwindled, I was forced to reconstruct the center of my dignity to be relieved of this burden and to relax. As Christ has given me a new image of myself, and a realistic assessment of my personal worth, the inner pull toward the limelight has lessened.

The "failure factor," which all of us possess to one degree or another, has caused me to weigh beforehand the considerations of my mind. I have participated in too many abortive pilgrimages (tremendous starts without a finish) to unveil my thoughts and intents naively. If this is fear of incompetence, then I choose fear of incompetence. I have seen myself in the mirror too often as that impetuous Simon Peter who dabbled endlessly with empty talk.

I chuckle now as I recall that short quip that a seminary roommate taught me: "When all is said and done, more is said than done." Will Rogers, the king of American political humor, called President Calvin Coolidge "Silent Cal." He said of him: "He don't say much, but when he do, he don't say much." As individuals or as the Christian community, we perhaps do well to imbibe that terse statement by Ralph W. Sockman: "Men of taste are repelled by those who talk too easily and glibly about their personal religion. Jesus, the gentleman, liked persons of reserve and rebuked the emptiness of words without works." [4]

More and more widely, we are allowing the Christian faith to become a kind of *verbal mysticism.* The center of religious experience is beginning to mean a matter of everyone simply expressing his faith from the standpoint of how he feels at any given moment in any given circle, however

---

[4] Ralph W. Sockman, *Recoveries in Religion* (Nashville, Tennessee: Cokesbury Press, 1938), p. 173.

naive and meaningless he may sound. Just to have something to say as verbosely as one can possibly say it seems to
be in vogue. Not unlike medieval mysticism, religion becomes based on the common denominator of *feeling* in varying types of emotional and intellectual sessions. We gather
in our groups without the least regard for gauging the quality
of our contribution to them. We get caught up into the
democracy of our own thoughts, and the spate of verbal
mysticism ends in a bad rash of monologue — which by the
way is not the most wholesome basis for growing honest and
open relationships. Indeed, there should be a balance between free speech and silence. Adlai Stevenson once remarked:

> I yield to no man in my belief in the principle of free
> debate. The sound of tireless voices is the price we pay
> for the right to hear the music of our own opinions. But
> there is also a moment at which democracy must prove
> its capacity to act. Every man has a right to be heard;
> but no man has the right to strangle democracy with a
> single set of vocal cords. [5]

There are countless jokes, which on the lighter side, poke
fun at the more voluble souls. One such joke is a magazine
filler entitled "Sound Advice." "Two women were chatting
in a restaurant booth. One seemed to have an endless tape
running through her voice box. Finally, the other said,
'Helen, why don't you take up Christian Silence?'" [6] Because
most of us, like Helen, can be grossly overbearing, we may
save ourselves some friends and a place to belong by listening to this sportive warning.

When one of our *koinonia* groups had ceased meeting on
a regular basis, Martha and Patsy — two regular participants
— entertained the idea of coming to see my wife and me.
We had joined in fellowship and mutual sharing around
our dining room table a number of times before. This time

[5] "Free Speech, Ltd.," *The Reader's Digest* (Feb., 1967), p. 106.
[6] Miriam Natkins, quoted by Norton Mockridge in New York *World
Journal Tribune*. Reprinted by *The Reader's Digest* (March, 1967), p. 87.

it was to be different — or so it was hoped. Martha said, "You realize, don't you, that every time we come to see you, we sit around that huge table and ask one another questions? I would like to come this time and, if nothing else, just look at you all."

"You know," she continued, "just be there!" Patsy joined the laughter as I invited them over for all the "looking" they desired.

Since then the occasion has become a standard joke, but I understood what Martha meant. Most of us are over-vocal, over-probing, and over-conspicuous. O. Hallesby, a one-time professor in the Independent Theological Seminary in Oslo, Norway, realized this. In a little book that went through forty-one editions, he made it plain that people who know one another really well can spend time in silence together — something that cannot be done with *others*. "We must converse with them," he says, "entertain them either with interesting or profound things as the case may be. With our own dear ones, however, we can speak freely about common and insignificant things. In their presence, too, we can be silent." [7]

If we must parade before men, perhaps we should choose the more gallant parade of silent dignity. A "silent dignity" is indeed a radical essential to creative silence. *We must possess it in the Christian community as a fourth enterprising lesson.* If we could better know who we are and recover an adequate sense of our dignity, we could more readily gain a security for the quiet pilgrimage. Only then could the community be personally effective in the world, as it would no longer be bound to the vain-glorious.

To take a tip from the One whose silent dignity spoke louder than His words, might aid the Christian community in actualizing its pervasive role. There was no great evangelistic fanfare with Christ. When He went out to minister, He liked the narrowness of a single soul in trouble. His only

[7] O. Hallesby, *Prayer*, trans. by Clarence J. Carlsen (Minneapolis, Minn.: Augsburg Publishing House, 1931 - 1947), pp. 147-48.

joy of expanse was the quietness of a hillside. He followed the philosophy of the "secret chamber" and taught others to do the same. He knew something about "the eyes of God which see in secret"; hands do not reveal the intent of the heart when it comes to giving; prayer is no announcement but a silent sojourn between the deepest self and God; fasting is no matter of "appearance" but a most inconspicuous time-loss to the mind when one is caught up into some priceless venture in life at the moment. [8]

There was a time when Christ's own brothers chided Him to go into Judea, especially around Jerusalem at the time of the traditional Jewish Feast of Tabernacles, where His display of works and ministry would really count. "No one who seeks to be in the limelight," they said, "does things where they are not observed. Since You do these things, show Yourself to the world." [9] Two cheap alternatives loomed before Him. In their estimate, He could either be an undercover man whose work would be done in abject secrecy, or He could be a publicity hound, espousing a spectacular role. To choose the former meant a divorcement from the world. To choose the latter meant to over-awe the people by calling attention to Himself. But Christ chose neither to shun the world nor to coerce it. He chose to be at home in the world, to be part of it, to share in its hurt, to give Himself openly, but to save Himself from the ridiculous.

For the moment, Christ stayed in Galilee and awaited the suitable time. When His brothers had gone to the feast, "He went also, not publicly but privately." [10] Even the Jews had expected a more public appearance, for they kept asking, "Where is He?" [11]

When the feast days were half over, Christ went up to the Temple to teach and there to test the initial response of the people. They were overwhelmed that a man out of such

---

[8] Sermon on the Mount, Matthew 6:1-18. See also John 4:31-34.
[9] John 7:3, 4 (The Modern Language Bible).
[10] John 7:10 (M.L.B.).
[11] John 7:11 (M.L.B.).

obscurity, having never studied in the Rabbinical schools, could know the Scripture. Here He tried to inform them, without celebration, that His teaching had the breath of another world. "Whoever utters merely his own ideas is seeking his own honor," He said, "but whoever seeks the honor of him who sent him is sincere, and there is no dishonesty in him." [12]

Men did not understand the nonclamorous, uncalculating mood with which Christ moved. That was quite unlike the Messiah for whom they looked. Some at the feast said, "We know where this person is from. When the Messiah comes no one will know where He is from." [13] Others rhetorically asked: "The Christ does not come from Galilee, does He? Does not the Scripture say that the Christ comes from the offspring of David and from Bethlehem, the town where David lived?" [14] The records showed that no real prophet had ever come from Galilee, especially from such an *insignificant* place as Nazareth. Still others questioned His destiny: "Where is He intending to go, so we cannot find Him? He surely does not plan to visit the Dispersion among the Greeks and to teach the Greeks?" [15] His going to the Dispersion among the heathen would be unthinkable to the orthodox Jew. Such could not be personally impressive. Yet, Christ involved Himself in the remote and insignificant elements of His day. He ministered to forgotten men, and He was misunderstood for it.

Christ waited in silence during the remainder of the feast until the last day, unimposingly awaiting His turn among the rabbis. An official envoy from the high priests, intending His capture, heard this Teacher and returned to the court with the words: "No man ever spoke as this man speaks." [16] When the officials could not break the riddle of Christ's

[12] John 7:18 (C. B. Wms.).
[13] John 7:27 (M.L.B.).
[14] John 7:41, 42 (M.L.B.).
[15] John 7:35 (M.L.B.).
[16] John 7:46 (M.L.B.).

authority, grasp His silent dignity, or understand His un-
assuming candor, the tribunal broke up and "every man went
to his own house." [17]

If there is anything the church needs in our day, it is
the hush of Christ. Our worship becomes regalia. Our evangelism smacks of the spectacular. Our daily walk suffers
from the lack of love toward those outside of Christ. Our
heartbeat is frantic, insecure, coercive. We are no lullaby to
souls in desperation. And the chief reason for it is that,
unlike Christ, we do not possess ourselves. We do not even
know ourselves. We are unsure, unprecise, vacuous. We are
doubtful of human dignity at large because we are uncertain
of our own. We make up for the lack by being boisterous,
overbearing, and theatrical. Of all peoples we are most de-
corous, most proud.

It is quite an anomaly that men feel they must amplify
their own worth by tying themselves to elite circumstances,
knowledgeable people, or self-assertive attitudes. There is no
greater example of this in the New Testament than the
Pharisees. Christ accused them of hitching their wagons to
a star in John the Baptist, in whose ministry they delighted
momentarily. For a time, John was a lamp burning brightly
and loudly acclaimed. The legalists rallied in support of his
rugged Essene manner. He was lauded as a man of prowess.
But when John revealed that he was just "a voice preaching
in the wilderness," they unhitched their wagons. They dared
not hitch their wagon to a "falling star." Christ, in turn,
never made His impact upon them, for in Him there was
not enough humanism. He did not recommend or extol
Himself. His chief sanction was a *silent testimony* — a testimony, He assured the Pharisees, "given by the Father who
sent me, although you never heard his voice or saw his
form." [18] But they needed a more human, tactile certifica-

---

[17] John 7:53 (k.j.v.).
[18] John 5:37. (The New English Bible). © The Delegates of Oxford
University Press and the Syndics of Cambridge University Press 1961, 1970.
Reprinted by permission.

tion, a more self-accrediting attitude. Christ went on to augment His pronouncement against their fondest wish:

> I do not look to men for honour. . . . I have come accredited by my Father and you have no welcome for me; if another comes self-accredited you will welcome him. How can you have faith so long as you receive honour from one another, and care nothing for the honour that comes from him who alone is God?[19]

Honor rests in the "image of God"; proof of it is in His character. Goodness, Christ said, roots in God and not in ourselves. A sense of dignity that rests in Him needs no further bolstering. It can act calmly or declaratively, and still be winsome. The Christian community, therefore, whether militant or mild, discovers its true dignity only when it is no longer self-accrediting. And this, undoubtedly, is the dynamism within silence. Dignity really needs no vocal proof.

A final and more practical means of achieving creative silence in community is through occasional "assemblies of silence." This procedure traditionally has been prescribed by the Society of Friends for their own worship experiences. Such a procedure, however, often meets with disapproval by those churches unsteeped in the Quaker doctrine of the "Inner Light." Whether this doctrine is adopted completely is inconsequential if one accepts the view that God indeed breaks into our silence without nurturing a Christian determinism. Apparently, this is the essential meaning held by many Quakers.

Almost a century and a half ago, the heralded Quaker, Robert Barclay, in vindicating the principles and doctrines of the Quakers, cited the following objection from those who opposed the Quaker form of worship: "It seems to be an unprofitable exercise," they said, "for a man to be doing or thinking nothing. . . ." Barclay responded to his critics by saying: "That is not unprofitable, which is of absolute neces-

[19] John 5:41, 43, 44 (N.E.B.).

sity before any other duty can be acceptably performed, as we have shown this waiting to be." [20]

The "presence" of Christ, "obedience" to His will, and "discipline," which prepare and strengthen the worshiper for his creative task in the world are the incisive elements to be learned in these "assemblies of silence." To learn these is to learn the chief lesson of all about creative silence; namely, that it shuns an impatient humanism and instead adopts the philosophy of waiting, which says, "if God permits."

[20] Robert Barclay, *An Apology for the True Christian Divinity* (New York: Samuel Wood and Sons, 1826), p. 382.

Chapter 14

If God Permits!

> "And we will progress, if God permits."
> — Hebrews 6:3 (C. B. Wms.)

I was about to leave his office and the consultation concerning my search for a new direction in the ministry, when my teacher added: "Remember, my dear friend, you can do anything you want to do!" I knew my teacher too well to think that he was speaking in humanistic terms. He was not suggesting in the least that I could support in my own Atlas strength whatever change was to come. Nor did he mean that I was adequately prepared for just any enterprising role in life. I credited this man with much more spiritual understanding than that. Something of the ring of "Jesus Christ" sounded at the heart of his statement. I took it to mean that this world is open to men of calm determination and steady drive who, under Jesus Christ, pursue deep values with intensity and adventure. The door closed behind me, and I walked away under the aura of a new discovery — "Life is open-ended when Jesus Christ is at its center!" Over and over that clause — "Life is open-ended" — made its impact.

Now I must confess my own exploitable humanity. I have not always looked at life as being open-ended. Something in me wants to languish, even since that aura-clad moment when I discovered life as an open-air adventure. Regretfully, it has not always been "adventure"; nor has it been even cold progress. To be honest, I look at life first as "obstacle." Only through the eyes of Christ do I see it as "opportunity." In this way I am like every other man: I "belong" to the human race with all its inhibiting frailty, its moral blindness, its picayune humanism.

Gratefully, the story does not end here. I am learning again that life bears no finalities. "The one fatal intellectual heresy is the heresy of finality. It is to assume that we have come to an end of the adventure of living, with our thinking done, a state of society fixed, a system of law that need not be altered, a theology that is sacred." [1] Life must have its pauses, its interruptions, even its profuse struggles that are certain to come. Life can handle the ominous, the precarious; but it cannot long endure its breathless moments when the heart no longer stirs at the excitable in the world. Nor can it bear up against the dry winds that sweep across man's shadowless plateaus.

Life must not level off. It must be invested, heightened, or diminishing returns set in. Then comes boredom! Then frustration! And then the hapless plunge toward the vacuous, the insane!

Life was meant to have color on an ascending scale. It was meant to have the shape of the fertile egg, opening into the infinite. It was meant to flow, to be always emerging, buttressed and forced upward.

In the study of genetics there is a principle, which, if properly understood, reveals a remarkable feature about life. The feature is that life is not merely process, not merely movement, but of necessity *advance*. The principle is called the "epigenetic principle," which technically means a "gradual diversification and differentiation" in the growth of any living entity. With reference to the pre-natal development of the human baby, the principle means that each stage of the fetus has a point of ascendancy. If the mother becomes

[1] Hugh Black, *The Adventure of Being Man* (Garden City, N. Y.: Doubleday, Doran & Company, Inc., 1929), p. 25.

seriously ill during any given point of ascendancy, the baby may be born with some weakness — weak eyes, weak heart, or any one or more of a host of other weaknesses. Life, to be healthy, must guarantee the safety of its advancing stages.

The Christian community, likewise, rather than setting finalities, must go beyond each advancing stage of its life. "Christianity is not a *status* at which one arrives; it is a *life* in which one matures." [2] This is essentially what the writer of *Hebrews* meant when writing to the second generation Hebrew Christians: "So then let us once for all quit the elementary teaching about Christ and continue progressing toward maturity; let us stop relaying a foundation of repentance from works that mean only death, and of faith in God, of teaching about ceremonial washings and the laying on of hands, the resurrection of the dead and final judgment. And we will progress, if God permits." [3]

The writer was not asking these Christians to become oblivious to the fundamentals of their faith. The call, on the contrary, was to proceed from the fundamentals, from the plateaus already established. To "progress" did not mean to "discard." Paul, himself, in writing to the Philippian Christians, recognized that to grow into maturity, "we must continue to live up to that degree of success that we have already reached." [4] The call of the writer of Hebrews and of Paul is the call to claim the growing-edge.

The growing-edge of Christianity is like an oasis in the desert. The grass, making its way from the source of its life near the pool, generates its own soil as it grows. The tendrils reach out into the burning sand, bringing with them the nutritive substance processed from the water. Two things are important for its survival: it must remain attached to its source and alive at its growing-edge.

These are the two points that I am suggesting in this

[2] Keith Miller, *The Taste of New Wine* (Waco, Texas: Word Books, 1965), p. 100.
[3] Hebrews 6:1-3 (C. B. Wms.).
[4] Philippians 3:16 (C. B. Wms.).

chapter. The church, to survive, must remain alive at its growing edge and attached to its source in the Living Christ. What is important is that the church possess "eternal life" *now!* Eternal life is not merely continuity beyond the grave; it is an ever-widening, ever-invigorating kind of life, evident only in Jesus Christ, that has *no saturation point.* Always something new is being added. The church must also have sustained hope for this New Life. We are certain not to have it unless we rest dogmatically in the One who possesses it and freely gives it away.

The writer of *Hebrews* thus counsels the Christian community to "press on toward maturity." The English translation, however, leaves us with the slight impression that we are to proceed in humanistic fashion. If this is our impression, it is obviously the wrong one when we discover that the passage from the Greek literally reads, "let us be borne along." Curiously, the word used here is the same word used in *Acts* to describe the fate of the ship of the Roman guard caught in a northeasterly gale off the coast of Crete. In the violent wind, the ship was snatched along until it could no longer bear the maelstrom. So the sailors on board had no alternative but to "let her drive." [5] This is precisely what the writer of *Hebrews* is suggesting in the case of the Christian community — let God drive! Paraphrasing it: "Let us be borne along toward maturity. . . . And this we will do (be borne along) if God permits."

Many generations have gone hep on the Man-Measure theory *(Homo Mensura)* in philosophy, which proposes that man is the measure of all things; that he needs no divine permit, no spiritual power, no sacred roots. From Protagoras, in whom such humanism began, to Feuerbach, in whom it was revived, man has freely extolled himself as the pole-star of the universe. Perhaps such men have never read, or perhaps they do not care to read, God's reprobation of the Prince of Tyrus: "Thus saith the Lord God: because

[5] Acts 27:15 (C. B. Wms.).

thine heart is lifted up, and thou hast said, I am a God, I sit in the seat of God, in the midst of the seas; yet thou art a man, and not God, though thou set thine heart as the heart of God." [6]

The influence of Feuerbach's irrationalism, with its central humanism, became the fountain-head of modern Communism. Communism views man as being shaped totally by a materialistic, mechanistic world. Marxist man is boastfully bound up in his own innate abilities. Within recent years, however, this doctrinaire human technology has been singled out by those who have supported it as an inadequate assumption concerning the nature of man. For instance, the fourth assembly of the World Council of Churches met in Uppsala, Sweden in 1968. One of its speakers, Dr. Josef Hromadka of Czechoslovakia, told the press that the Marxist intellectuals were discovering that their theories could not answer the deep questions regarding the nature of man. They were thus turning to Christianity for the answers. They were finding that man is more than psycho-social, geo-political, and historico-economic in nature.

After Marx came Charles Darwin with *The Origin of Species.* His central evolutionary concept was "the survival of the fittest," in which man endlessly struggles for his place — and struggles alone.

Not long after, Friedrich Wilhelm Nietzsche put the capstone on humanism with his emphasis on "the will to power." Man must struggle to the summit of life by his own "will to power." He must become his own "Superman," to use Nietzsche's term, because "God is dead!" In his dying hour, Nietzsche, racked with insanity, faintly remarked: "Do we not feel the breath of void in our faces? Isn't it growing colder? Is not night always coming on, one night after another, more and more?"

Nietzsche's "Superman" sparked in the mind of Hitler in Germany and he dreamed of a superior race who would

[6] Ezekiel 28:2 (K.J.V.).

govern the world. If men wanted a "God" he would give them one — the German Fuehrer! If men wanted a cause, he would supply that too — the German state! We need not cite the insolence of Nazism and the horrible spoils of World War II, which resulted. We need only to admit that man, "the measure of all things," is dead!

If the Christian church, in its pursuit of growth and renewal, is ever tempted to "call its own shots," then I hope it will read the history of *humanism.* Afterward, I hope it will read for comparison Paul's first prayer made in behalf of the Christians at Ephesus:

> . . . that the God of our Lord Jesus Christ, the glorious Father, may grant you the Spirit to give wisdom and revelation which come through a growing knowledge of Him, by having the eyes of your hearts enlightened, so that you may know what the hope is to which He calls you, how gloriously rich God's portion in His people is, and how surpassingly great is His power for us who believe, *measured* by His tremendously mighty power when He raised Christ from the dead, and seated Him at His right hand in heaven, far above every other government, authority, power, and dominion, yea, far above every other title that can be conferred, not only in this world but in the world to come. And so He has put all things under His feet and made Him the supreme Head of the church, which is His body, that is being filled by Him who fills everything everywhere. [7]

If God not only sanctions the renewal and progress of the church, but is also the *measure* of that renewal and that progress, then we hardly dare to proceed on anything but His grace, His presence.

The great Methodist missionary, E. Stanley Jones, has reminded us that "organized Christianity" has often blocked reform; "but wherever it has turned to its Fountain Head, Christ," he continues, "it has been awakened to reform. . . . The non-Christian faiths carry on reform as they move away

[7] Ephesians 1:17-23 (C. B. Wms.). Italics are mine.

from their base, the Christian faith as it moves toward its base." [8] This was in 1928. Now, forty years later, in his spiritual autobiography, *A Song of Ascents,* Jones gives us the very same maxim: "As long as you have Jesus Christ in any group, you have a center of possible revival and renewal." [9]

Combined with that heartening aphorism is the perceptiveness, also, of the late Harry Emerson Fosdick, who wrote: "All the vital reformations in the Christian church have had one common element: the religion of Jesus has pushed its way up through the obscurities and formalities of an accumulated religion concerning him and has taken once more the center of the scene." [10]

The real question for the Christian community, then, is not the divine side but the human. Granted that the church cannot proceed unless God permits, it must now ask whether *it has in itself the will to renewal.* Jesus Christ is more than furniture among His people. He is ready to lead us into renewed life in the church if we are ready to follow. Through Paul the church may be assured of "the power of His resurrection." It may know that it may be "continuously transformed by His death." What it now needs to know is whether, with Paul, it will press on to capture that ideal for which it was captured by Christ Jesus. It must now entertain whether it is ready to surrender the past and receive what the future holds — "the prize to which God through Jesus Christ is calling us upward." [11]

We have made at least a start when we have refused finality for a more current gospel. Perhaps the miracle of renewal will happen when the church understands more fully the principles that comprise its life. Being carved, as they are, out of a long history of the acts of God, they may

[8] E. Stanley Jones, *Christ at the Roundtable* (London: Hodder and Stoughton, Limited, 1928), p. 57.

[9] E. Stanley Jones, *A Song of Ascents: A Spiritual Autobiography* (Nashville: Abingdon Press, 1968), p. 272.

[10] Harry Emerson Fosdick, *Adventurous Religion* (New York: Blue Ribbon Books, 1926), p. 311.

[11] See Philippians 3:10-15 (C. B. Wms.).

now be etched into the contemporary moral fabric of the church. From the human side, it may be true that the church will have renewed "community" by *paying* for it rather than by *reaching* for it, but from the divine side, it is equally true that it will be a *gift* and not a *transaction*. What really counts at last is what God does, not what we do.

In the meantime, somewhere among all this, there is a place to belong for everyone — a place for the alienated, the lonely, the disconsolate, as well as for the man who struggles for a more honorable Christian commitment. My prayer for these is the prayer of Micah for Israel:

> O shepherd, guide thy people, thine own flock,
> so lonely, lonely like a wild patch within a garden.
>
> — Micah 7:14 (Moffatt)

Index

A

Acceptance, 34, 54, 96, 99, 108
Affirmation, 32ff, 94, 102, 145
Agape, 73 - 79, 100
Alaska, 117
Alcoholic, 36
Aloneness, 87
Apologetics, 31
Ashdod, 130
Augustine, St., 64
Availability, 127ff

B

Bankruptcy, Spiritual, 81 - 84, 88,
  90 - 91, 111
Barbarism, 107
Barclay, Robert, 163 - 64
Behanna, Gert, 76
Belonging, 17f, 30, 35, 42, 46, 64 -
  65, 108, 134, 145ff
"Ben Hur," 23
Black, Hugh, 166
Bliss, Kathleen, 105
Bonhoeffer, Dietrich, 87, 92, 102 -
  103, 116
Bribery, 74f
Brunner, Emil, 69, 70

C

Caesarea, 130
Carey, William, 127
Carnell, Edward J., 29, 32
Carver, W. O., 131
Cenchreae, 133
Center, 71, 73ff
Christ, 23ff, 35, 39, 47, 81, 93-96,
  103, 114f, 117, 123, 129, 160 - 64
Christian, 19, 105f
Christianity, 21 - 22, 57, 59, 71, 117
Church —
  Body of Christ, 106, 110

"Family of God," 58
  Institutional, 57, 59, 63, 67, 106
  Local, 18 - 19, 106
  Organism, 110
  Organization, 110
  "People of God," 38, 61, 66
  "Temple of God," 58
Churchill, Winston, 134, 135
Circumcision, Symbol of, 67 - 68, 144
Circumference, Spiritual, 71ff
Clark, Glenn, 142
Commitment, 115, 133
Communication, 105, 110
Communism, 135, 138 - 139, 169, see
  also Dialectical Materialism
Community —
  Christian, 83, 89 - 90, 93, 103,
    108 - 109, 147, 167f
  · House-Church, 58ff, 68ff, 133, 150
Compassion, 77
Conversion, 21 - 22, 90
Coolidge, Calvin, 157
Corinth, 83, 100
Covenant, 67
Cynicism, 116 - 17

D

Darwin, Charles, 169
Davis, Creath, 107, 141
Deacon, 130ff
Deception, 43, 45, 47, 55, 86, 90
Defeat, 82, 88, 152 - 53
Deification, False, 155 - 57
"Democracy-in-Action," 138
Dependent, 107
Determinism, 114, 125, 163
Diakonia, 130ff
Dialogue, 50, 80, 140ff
Dignity, 49, 86, 113, 159ff, 162
Dilemma, Moral, 86
Discipline, 75 - 76, 80
Dreaming, 135ff

173

E

Einstein, Albert, 26
Electrolysis, 120
Elijah, 23
"Epigenetic Principle," 166
Estrangement, 87
Exaggeration, 43

F

Faith, 143
Fellowship, 29ff
Fénelon, François, 99
Feuerbach, 168 - 69
Flattery, 33
Forgiveness, 36ff, 52, 91ff
Form, Church, 56ff
Freedom, 82
Friendship, 17ff, 54, 93, 96, 122

G

Gayle, Johnny, 127
God, Image of, 86
Gospels, 31
Grace, 95
Graham, Billy, 22, 127
Gray, Jack, 110
Groups, *Koinonia*, 32f, 60 - 62
Growth, Christian, 153f
Guilt, 37, 94 - 95

H

Hadden, Jeffrey K., 109
Hallesby, O., 159
Healing, 92ff, 104
Hendry, George S., 107
Hitler, Adolf, 169 - 70
Hoekendijk, J. C., 61, 64, 132
Honesty, 47
Hromadka, Josef, 169
Humanism, 114, 162, 164, 165ff
Humanity, 69, 81, 164
Hypocrite, 43, 45, 49, 86

I

Indispensability, 116ff
Indulgence, 75, 96, 115
Inferiority, 89
Intercession, 103
Involvement, 103, 110
Irresponsibility, 94

J

Jefferson, Charles E., 63
Jeremiah, 24
John the Baptist, 24
Jones, E. Stanley, 156, 170, 171
Joseph, 97
Judaism, 57 - 59, 66, 130
Judgment, Unbridled, 88, 89 - 90
Justice, 75, 93 - 96

K

Kaléo Lodge, 34, 142
Kennedy, Robert F., 136
Koinonia, 32f, 50, 61, 80, 83, 88, 140

L

Lagemann, John Kord, 144
Lay Training Center, 140ff
Light, 116ff
Listening, 144ff
Livingston, David, 127
Lord, 87
Love, 68ff, 95, 96, 97, 100, 113
Lucifer, 85

M

MacArthur, General Douglas, 138
Madden, Myron, 105 - 106
Magnetism, Spiritual, 122 - 23
Malik, Charles, 138
Mansfield, Katherine, 42
Marx, Karl, 135, 169
Materialism, Dialectical, 135
Matthew, 48
Maturity, 168
May, Rollo, 88, 109
Menninger, Karl, 108
Mercy, 75, 96, 115
Methodology, 124
Miller, Keith, 154, 167
Moralism, 79, 121, 124
Mullen, Thomas J., 148
Mysticism, Verbal, 157

N

Narcissus, 112
Nazism, 170
Nietzsche, Friedrich Wilhelm, 169
Nimkoff, Meyer F., 108
Norm, 45ff, 62

O

Obedience, 83
Ogburn, William F., 108
Openness, 42ff, 63
Osborne, Cecil G., (Foreword), 99 - 100
Other-centered, 87

P

Pagan, 117
Panacea, Spiritual, 102f
Pardon, 92 - 93, 103
Parker, William R., 101, 146
Paul, the Apostle, 38, 47
People, of God, 62, 66 - 67
Philia, 71-73, 78-79
Philip, 129 - 30
Phoebe, 133
Pilgrimage, 81
Pity, 77, 97
Poverty, 127 - 28
Prayer, 136ff
Preservation, Spiritual, 80ff
Pretense, 21, 44, 53 - 54
Pride, Spiritual, 88, 89
Primitive, 107
Prisoner, 92f, 149
Privacy, 63, 87, 105ff
Prodigal, 101
Property, 56
Protagoras, 168
Psychology, 72

Q

Quakers, 163 - 64

R

Reality, 27 - 28, 31, 34, 42, 48, 50 - 51
Reinforcement, 35
Relationships, 107f
Remorse, 103
Renewal, Church, 62, 81
Repentance, 50, 97 - 98
Resurrection, 29
Retreat, 82
Revenge, 103
Rogers, Will, 157
Roosevelt, Franklin D., 134

S

Salt, 116ff
Samaria, 94, 130
Saviour, 38
Schisgall, Oscar, 78
Self-gratification, 111
Self-life, 82, 84, 88, 90
Self-nihilism, 88
Servanthood, 27, 38 - 39, 40, 54, 111ff
Silence, 150ff
Simile, 116, 119
Simplicianus, 64
Sin, 21, 84 - 88
Skepticism, 29
Sociologists, 108, 109
Sockman, Ralph W., 157
Soliloquy, 39
Spontaneity, 113f, 125
Spurgeon, Charles Haddon, 56, 64, 95
Steinzor, Bernard, 32
Stevenson, Adlai, 158
Stevenson, Robert Louis, 152
Stewardship, 153
Struggle, 80, 83
Success, 82
Suffering, Fellowship of, 37ff
Sufficiency, Self-, 86, 89
Superiority, Feelings of, 33, 82, 89
Symbolism, 40

T

Testament, 104 - 105
Therapy, Prayer, 111, 146, 156
Thielicke, Helmut, 100
Tillich, Paul, 85, 95
Tournier, Paul, 90, 93, 97, 111 - 12, 145 - 46
Tracy, Nat, 43, 50, 83, 84, 85, 125
Transformation, 18, 22 - 23, 26, 93, 103
Trueblood, D. Elton, 83

U

Unconditionalism, 74 - 75, 95, 96 - 102
Unreality, 54 - 55